AF679147

The Confidence to Act: 30 Reflections on Data Governance

What Breaks and What Holds

KARIMA MAKROF

Technics Publications
SEDONA, ARIZONA

TECHNICS PUBLICATIONS

115 Linda Vista, Sedona, AZ 86336 USA
https://www.TechnicsPub.com

Edited by Steve Hoberman
Cover design by Lorena Molinari

All rights reserved. No part of this book may be reproduced or transmitted in any form or by any means, electronic or mechanical, including photocopying, recording, or by any information storage and retrieval system, without written permission from the publisher, except for brief quotations in a review.

The authors and publisher have taken care in the preparation of this book, but make no expressed or implied warranty of any kind and assume no responsibility for errors or omissions. No liability is assumed for incidental or consequential damages in connection with or arising out of the use of the information or programs contained herein.

All trade and product names are trademarks, registered trademarks, or service marks of their respective companies and are the property of their respective holders and should be treated as such.

Without in any way limiting the author's exclusive rights under copyright, any use of this publication to "train" generative artificial intelligence (AI) technologies to generate text is expressly prohibited. The author reserves all rights to license uses of this work for generative AI training and the development of machine learning language models.

First Printing 2026

Copyright © 2026 by Karima Makrof

ISBN, print ed. 9798898160883
ISBN, Kindle ed. 9798898160890
ISBN, PDF ed. 9798898160906

Library of Congress Control Number: 2026938454

For my children, Gillian, Elliot and Tilly -
and for all those who choose to act, even when certainty is out of reach.

Acknowledgments

This book was shaped through conversations, challenges, and practice.

My thanks to Bob Seiner for his early support and guidance as this project took form.

To Sandrine, for her friendship and steady support throughout.

To my parents, for everything that made this possible.

And to my children, for the energy, perspective, and constant reminder of what matters most.

Endorsements

Karima is someone who gets it. She has worked tirelessly in data governance and shares her experiences with others to help them learn and take responsibility for their data. She has developed a book around solving issues that impact confidence in data. Without that confidence, people are second-guessing their decisions, or worse, failing to act at all.

Merrill Albert, Data Evangelist

Karima brings a practical and experienced voice to data governance. In this book, she reflects on the realities organizations face when trying to make governance work, and why it so often breaks down when pressure rises. What makes this book especially useful is its focus on the decisions, behaviors, and everyday moments that determine whether governance holds in practice. Any practitioner serious about building governance that lasts, and supports better decisions, will find this book worth reading more than once.

Håkan Edvinsson
Data management advisor, author of *Data Diplomacy*

Karima has written a book that genuinely meets people where they are in their relationship with data, growth, and self-awareness, and then gently but effectively moves them forward. What stood out to me most is how her "30 reflections" create space for people to pause, think, and reconnect with what really matters, while still nudging them toward action. In the work I have done, I often say that real change does not begin with mandates, it begins with recognition and awareness of what is already happening. Karima captures that same spirit beautifully. She recognizes that people are already thinking, already feeling, and already behaving in ways that can be shaped into something more intentional and impactful. This book does not try to force change. It acts as a catalyst for it.

What I appreciate even more is how practical and relatable the content is without ever feeling heavy-handed. The reflections encourage readers to move beyond passive thinking and into meaningful shifts in behavior, which is where true value is realized. Whether we are talking about governing data or guiding personal growth, the outcome is the same. Clarity leads to better decisions, and better decisions lead to better outcomes. Karima's work reinforces the idea that small, thoughtful moments can spark significant progress when they are connected to purpose and consistency. This is a book that will resonate with a wide audience because it respects where people are, while helping them see where they can go next.

Robert S. Seiner
President & Principal – KIK Consulting & Educational Services

Contents

Foreword 7

Introduction 11
How to Use This Book 14
How Each Chapter Is Structured 15
Three Principles 16
A Note on the Examples 17
A Note on Language 18

Part 1: Why Data Governance Matters 19

Day 1: The Foundation of Trusted Insights 21
From the 30 Days of Data Governance Posts 22
Looking Back From Practice 23

Day 2: Clear Ownership and Accountability 27
From the 30 Days of Data Governance Posts 28
Looking Back From Practice 29

Day 3: Data Quality Is Queen 31
From the 30 Days of Data Governance Posts 32
Looking Back From Practice 33

Day 4: Data Flows and Processes 37
From the 30 Days of Data Governance Posts 38
Looking Back From Practice 39

Day 5: The Cost of Bad Data 43
From the 30 Days of Data Governance Posts 44
Looking Back From Practice 45

Part 1 Your Turn 47

Part 2: Building a Strong Foundation ___ 49

Day 6: Roles and Responsibilities ___ 51
From the 30 Days of Data Governance Posts ___ 52
Looking Back From Practice ___ 53

Day 7: Policies and Standards ___ 57
From the 30 Days of Data Governance Posts ___ 58
Looking Back From Practice ___ 59

Day 8: Data Definitions and Glossary ___ 63
From the 30 Days of Data Governance Posts ___ 64
Looking Back From Practice ___ 65

Day 9: Information Architecture ___ 69
From the 30 Days of Data Governance Posts ___ 70
Looking Back From Practice ___ 71

Day 10: Simple Metrics and KPIs ___ 75
From the 30 Days of Data Governance Posts ___ 76
Looking Back From Practice ___ 77

Part 2 Your Turn ___ 81

Part 3: Avoiding Common Pitfalls ___ 83

Day 11: Data Silos ___ 85
From the 30 Days of Data Governance Posts ___ 86
Looking Back From Practice ___ 88

Day 12: Manual Processes vs Automation ___ 91
From the 30 Days of Data Governance Posts ___ 92
Looking Back From Practice ___ 93

Day 13: Missing Data and Gaps ___ 97
From the 30 Days of Data Governance Posts ___ 98
Looking Back From Practice ___ 99

Day 14: Conflicting Sources **103**
From the 30 Days of Data Governance Posts 104
Looking Back From Practice 105

Day 15: Inconsistent Processes **107**
From the 30 Days of Data Governance Posts 108
Looking Back From Practice 109

Part 3 Your Turn **113**

Part 4: Embedding Governance in Daily Work **115**

Day 16: Data Stewardship **117**
From the 30 Days of Data Governance Posts 118
Looking Back From Practice 119

Day 17: Audit and Validation **123**
From the 30 Days of Data Governance Posts 124
Looking Back From Practice 125

Day 18: Reporting and Dashboards **129**
From the 30 Days of Data Governance Posts 130
Looking Back From Practice 131

Day 19: Communication and Collaboration **133**
From the 30 Days of Data Governance Posts 134
Looking Back From Practice 135

Day 20: Training and Awareness **139**
From the 30 Days of Data Governance Posts 140
Looking Back From Practice 141

Part 4 Your Turn **145**

Part 5: Advanced Practices and Strategic Impact 149

Day 21: Master Data Management 151
From the 30 Days of Data Governance Posts 152
Looking Back From Practice 154

Day 22: Metadata and Lineage 157
From the 30 Days of Data Governance Posts 158
Looking Back From Practice 159

Day 23: Data Privacy and Compliance 163
From the 30 Days of Data Governance Posts 164
Looking Back From Practice 165

Day 24: Data Governance Technology 169
From the 30 Days of Data Governance Posts 170
Looking Back From Practice 172

Day 25: Continuous Improvement 175
From the 30 Days of Data Governance Posts 176
Looking Back From Practice 178

Part 5 Your Turn 181

Part 6: Connecting Governance to Business Value 185

Day 26: Faster, Smarter Decisions 187
From the 30 Days of Data Governance Posts 188
Looking Back From Practice 190

Day 27: Reducing Risk and Cost 193
From the 30 Days of Data Governance Posts 194
Looking Back From Practice 195

Day 28: Strategic Alignments 199
From the 30 Days of Data Governance Posts 200
Looking Back From Practice 201

Day 29: Building a Data-Driven Culture **205**
From the 30 Days of Data Governance Posts 207
Looking Back From Practice 208

Day 30: The Road Ahead **213**
From the 30 Days of Data Governance Posts 214
Looking Back From Practice 215

Part 6 Your Turn **221**

Conclusion **223**
A Practical Roadmap 224
From Governance to Confidence 225

Closing: Governance as a Way of Working **227**

Appendix 1: The Six Parts: What Each One Builds **231**

Appendix 2: Where to Go When **235**

Appendix 3: Hashtags Used in 30 Days of Data Governance **237**

About the Author **243**

Index **245**

Foreword

In my years as Founder of Hyperight and Editorial Director behind platforms such as the Data Innovation Summit and Data 2030 Summit, I have had the privilege of engaging with thousands of practitioners, leaders, and organizations working at the forefront of data, analytics, and AI. Across these interactions, one truth has remained constant.

Every meaningful decision and every intelligent system depends on data, and on trust in that data.

Over the past two decades, I have witnessed the evolution of the field, from business intelligence to advanced analytics, machine learning, and artificial intelligence. Technologies have evolved rapidly, but the foundation has remained the same. Reliable, well-understood data is what enables systems to function and decisions to deliver value.

At the same time, I have seen how difficult this is to achieve in practice.

As organizations scale and data environments become more complex, governance is often either over-engineered into rigid structures or avoided altogether due to perceived overhead. Yet without it, the promise of data and AI cannot be realized.

This is why this book matters.

I have had the pleasure of working with Karima Makrof through multiple industry platforms, where she has contributed as both a speaker and moderator. What stands out in her work is a combination of clarity, discipline, and practicality. Her approach reflects a structured way of working, where complex challenges are broken down into manageable steps and continuously improved.

That philosophy is reflected throughout this book.

The Confidence to Act takes a grounded and practical approach to data governance. Rather than focusing on abstract frameworks, it breaks down the topic into essential components that can be applied in everyday work. The structure, built around focused reflections, encourages the reader to engage, assess, and take action.

What makes this book particularly valuable is its accessibility.

It is not written only for seasoned practitioners, but for anyone trying to understand data management and governance, with all its opportunities and challenges. It is stripped of false promises. Honest, immersive, and easy to engage with.

Beyond understanding, the book helps practitioners evaluate where they stand across ownership, data quality, processes, and organizational alignment, and what they need to do next. It provides a clear way to think, assess, and act.

Importantly, it reinforces a message that is often overlooked.

Data governance is not about control. It is about enabling confidence. Confidence in data, in decisions, and in the actions organizations take based on that data.

With that confidence, organizations can move faster, make better decisions, and unlock real value from their data.

I am pleased to recommend this book.

Goran Cvetanovski
Founder & CEO, Hyperight
Editorial Director, Data Innovation Summit and
Data 2030 Summit

Introduction

Why write a book about data governance?

There are many books, articles, frameworks, and posts about it. Many people seem to have discovered the discipline recently. For me, it has been part of my work for a long time, across financial services, logistics, retail, manufacturing, and technology organizations, in roles ranging from advisor and leader to embedded practitioner.

Most of these books attempt to answer the question "*How do we implement data governance?*" The question organizations were actually asking was different. It was quieter, more human, and it kept coming back regardless of industry or size:

Can we trust our data enough to act on it?

This book answers that question, not through another framework, but through thirty reflections drawn from practice, exploring the moments where data governance either quietly works or quietly breaks down.

Over time, I noticed something consistent: I kept receiving the same questions. Different organizations, different industries, different roles, but surprisingly similar questions about:

- Ownership.
- Trust in the numbers.

- Why data governance initiatives looked good on paper but somehow struggled once the real work started.

The answers were never exactly the same, of course. Context always matters. But the patterns were remarkably consistent.

That is what led to the original series.

One day, I simply decided to write some of those reflections down. The idea was to publish a short post every weekday on LinkedIn. Thirty days of thoughts about data governance, one reflection at a time. Small pieces of experience, shared in sequence. At the same time, I had just started my own company and was speaking with many organizations facing similar governance challenges. Those conversations reinforced the same observation: the questions may vary in wording, but the underlying issues tend to repeat.

What started as a writing exercise quickly became something else. People recognized their own situations in the examples. Conversations started. Others shared their own stories, frustrations, and lessons.

Because data governance rarely fails for the reasons people expect. It does not usually fail because organizations do not care about data. And it rarely fails because the framework was incomplete.

More often, data governance struggles because organizations try to fix complexity with structure instead of changing how decisions are made in everyday work.

That realization sits behind this book. Rather than write another framework-heavy governance manual, I wanted to capture the practical situations that organizations face: responsibility for data quality, how governance works once the policies are written, and how trust in data holds or fails in everyday work.

Each chapter reflects on one of those moments. Some are about structure: ownership, roles, processes. Some are about behavior: trust, communication, responsibility. All of them come from situations that organizations eventually face.

This is not a step-by-step implementation for rolling out data governance in thirty days. It is thirty reflections on what governance looks like when it is working, and what it reveals about organizations when it is not.

You can read the chapters sequentially, following the path from foundations to more advanced topics. Or you can dip in as situations arise in your own work. Either way, the intention is simple: to make data governance feel less like a framework to implement, and more like a way of working.

Governance is not about controlling data.

It is about enabling confidence.

Trust is what you feel about data. Confidence is what allows you to act. That is the idea this book is built around. Everything else follows from it.

How to Use This Book

This book is designed to be flexible. Each chapter explores one practical aspect of data governance, based on situations that organizations commonly encounter. You can approach it in several ways, depending on your needs and context:

- **Follow the original pace:** Read one chapter a day, as the series was originally designed. One reflection per weekday. This mirrors the rhythm of the LinkedIn series and gives each topic space to settle before the next one arrives. It is a useful pace if you want to bring data governance thinking into your routine rather than consume it all at once.

- **Read straight through:** The chapters follow a logical sequence: from understanding why data governance matters, through building foundations and avoiding pitfalls, to embedding data governance and connecting it to business value. If you are new to data governance, experienced in the discipline, or building a program from scratch, reading in order gives you a coherent arc. But each chapter is self-contained. If you read them out of sequence, nothing is lost. The sequence is an invitation, not a requirement.

- **Start with your biggest problem:** If a particular issue is already pressing in your organization, such as unclear ownership, data quality, stewardship, automation, or conflicting data sources, begin there and jump directly to the relevant day or part. Each chapter is designed to stand alone whilst connecting to the broader framework. Use the table of contents to find your pressure point.

- **Use as a reference:** Return to individual chapters when similar situations arise in your own data governance work. Keep this book nearby and turn to the relevant sections as needed. When ownership disputes emerge, revisit Days 2 and 6. When automation decisions loom, go back to Day 12. When data governance feels stuck, check Day 25 on continuous improvement. The consistent chapter structure makes it easy to find your way.

- **Discuss with your team:** Many readers will find this book most valuable when used collaboratively. Pick a chapter per week for team discussion. Let the "Looking Back From Practice" sections open the conversation, and share the challenges and reflections that resonate the most with your context. The "Your Turn" sections are designed to help you, the reader, pause and reflect on your own current situation. Use them thoughtfully. Share them. Build on what emerges.

How Each Chapter Is Structured

Every chapter follows the same three-part format. *Setting the context* opens with a brief framing of why the topic matters and how it connects to what came before. It is basically the "why this, why now" before diving in. *From the 30 Days of Data Governance Posts,* reproduce the original LinkedIn posts, lightly edited for length and clarity, but keeping their direct, conversational tone. *Looking Back From Practice* is where the reflection deepens, drawing on real experience to show what actually happens in organizations, where things go well, and where they go wrong.

Knowing this structure means you can also read selectively. If you want the quick take, the original post stands alone. If you want the fuller picture, the surrounding sections add the context and the lived reality behind it. Your choice. Your pace.

You do not need to read the chapters in order. But if you do, you may notice a pattern emerging: from understanding why trust in data breaks down, to recognizing how data governance becomes embedded in everyday work.

Three Principles

Three principles quietly run through every chapter of this book. They are worth naming before you begin, even if they simply accompany you rather than ask for your attention:

- **Keep it simple.** Data governance that grows too complex loses the people it depends on. The examples in this book are not about perfect designs; they are about finding the minimum clarity needed to move forward.

- **Keep it visible.** Ownership, quality, and accountability only work when they can be seen. Data governance that lives in documents but not in decisions does not really exist.

- **Keep it connected to what matters.** Every data governance effort outlined in this book is anchored to a decision, a cost, or a loss of confidence that someone felt. If that practice cannot be connected to something an organization actually needs to do, it is worth questioning.

These are not rules. They are the patterns I have seen in every organization where governance eventually worked.

A Note on the Examples

Throughout each chapter, you will find real-world examples in the "Looking Back From Practice" section. These are drawn from personal experience, including former clients I have worked with, organizations I have been part of, and companies I have advised over the years. Details have been adjusted where necessary to preserve confidentiality, but the situations, dynamics, and outcomes are real. The intention is not to describe specific organizations or proof points, but to illustrate patterns that recur across contexts and industries.

If they resonate, it is probably because you have seen something similar.

A Note on Language

Throughout this book, I sometimes use governance as shorthand for data governance. The context is always data, but the patterns, how decisions get made, how accountability is assigned, how trust is built, often apply more broadly than data alone.

Start small, be consistent,
and let trust compound over time.

PART 1

Why Data Governance Matters

Before frameworks, roles, or tools, there is a more fundamental question every organization eventually confronts:

Can we trust our data enough to act on it?

This first part exists to anchor the entire journey in that question because everything that follows depends on it. It is a deceptively simple question. Every organization has data. Many have more than they can use. And yet the honest answer, for a surprising number of them, is: not always. Not confidently. Not without checking first.

This part does not try to "sell" data governance. It surfaces why data governance becomes unavoidable as complexity grows. Organizations that resist it longest tend to pay the highest price, because what appears to be a data problem is almost always a decision problem in disguise.

When trust erodes, organizations compensate with manual checks, parallel numbers, and defensive behavior. Reports are questioned before they are used. Decisions slow as teams validate inputs rather than discuss implications. In many cases, the underlying problem is not the data alone, but a broken process that no longer supports how the organization actually works.

The chapters in this part establish the baseline: why trust matters, how it breaks, and why rebuilding it requires more than tools or good intentions. They reflect recurring patterns across organizations of different sizes and industries: unclear ownership, uneven quality, and data flows that no longer align with the business reality.

Without this foundation, every initiative that follows becomes heavier and more fragile. With it in place, governance becomes easier to rely on: not as an initiative to push forward, but as part of how the organization makes decisions.

At this stage, the goal is not to solve governance. It is to recognize it. To see where trust is already breaking, and why that matters more than any framework.

This part lays the ground beneath the entire book.

Day 1

The Foundation of Trusted Insights

I have rarely seen governance take hold when it arrives as a framework first. It works when organizations introduce it as an answer to a very human question:

> *Can we trust our data enough to act without second-guessing ourselves?*

Organizations do not *decide* to have poor data. They arrive there slowly, almost unintentionally. A workaround here. A manual correction there. A decision made "good enough for now". Until it no longer was.

Numbers start getting double-checked. Reports get questioned before they are discussed. Meetings spend more time debating inputs than discussing outcomes. A product launch discussion that should take thirty minutes runs to two hours because three people arrive with three different versions of the same sales figure. At some point, someone names it. Not as a strategic ambition. Not because it feels inspiring or exciting. But because the fatigue finally has a name: data governance.

Day 1 exists to ground the entire journey in that question. The answer rarely sits in theory or tooling alone, but in the lived experience of organizations trying to move forward while dragging uncertainty behind them.

From the 30 Days of Data Governance Posts

Over the next month, I will share insights, stories, and practical tips to help organizations turn messy, inconsistent, or hard-to-trust data into a strategic asset.

But first, what is data governance? In simple terms, it is the framework, rules, and accountability that ensure your data is accurate, consistent, and used responsibly. It is about giving your organization trustworthy data to make confident decisions.

In even simpler terms, it is a set of rules and ways to keep your data safe, correct, and easy to use. Like keeping kids' toys organized so you can always find the one you need. Only here it is the organization's information.

Why focus on it? Because data is at the heart of every decision. Without a strong foundation, even the best strategy is like building a house on sand. Errors creep in, processes break down, and confidence in decisions dwindles.

Good data governance is not just rules or policies. It is about creating trust, clarity, and alignment across your organization. It is the compass that ensures every department, every decision, every action is guided by reliable information.

Over this series, I will explore topics like:

- How to assign clear ownership and accountability.
- Quick wins that create visible impact.
- The connection between trusted data and confident decision-making.

Looking Back From Practice

What organizations often overlook is that trust in data is not binary.

It does not suddenly appear because a policy was approved, a strategy published, or a tool was purchased. Trust is built or weakened through everyday interactions: when a number changes without explanation, when two dashboards tell different stories, when no one can confidently answer *where the data comes from.*

In those moments, people adapt. They create parallel spreadsheets. They rely on "their version" of the data. They stop escalating issues because it feels pointless.

This is not resistance. It is pure and simple self-preservation. I have seen this pattern repeat in organizations of every size and sector, from a 50-person scale-up where one analyst had become the unofficial single source of truth, to multinationals where entire divisions had quietly stopped trusting the central data warehouse. The trigger is always the same: a small erosion of trust, a workaround, and then another workaround built on top of the first.

Example: *A retail organization I worked with had three different "customer count" numbers circulating simultaneously. Marketing used web analytics, Finance used billing records, and Operations used CRM data. Each department defended its number as "correct." The real problem was not technical. It was that no one had defined what "customer" meant for decision-making purposes. Once they agreed that "active customer" meant "purchased in the last 90 days," all three teams could reconcile their numbers. The technical fix took two days. Getting agreement on the definition took three months, but that agreement was what actually restored trust.*

Data governance, when done well, reverses this pattern. It reduces friction and makes the right behavior easier: fewer assumptions, fewer hand-offs, fewer debates about basics. It gives teams something extremely valuable: permission to move forward with confidence.

This is why governance should never be positioned as overhead. Its real value is speed with safety, enabling decisions that are both fast *and* defensible.

Day 1 comes *before* ownership, quality, processes, or tooling for a reason. If the organization does not share a clear understanding of *why* governance matters, every later effort becomes harder: ownership feels political, standards feel restrictive, metrics feel punitive.

When the "why" is clear, every element that follows, ownership, quality, processes, metrics, or tooling, becomes an enabler rather than a burden. This day sets the baseline mindset for everything that comes next: governance is not about perfection. It is about **reliability over time**.

Reliability is what allows organizations to grow, scale, and make decisions without constantly looking over their shoulder.

A note for those who want the shortest possible version: data governance is about who gets to decide what, when, and under which circumstances, as it relates to data. Every framework, role, and tool in the pages that follow is in service of that one idea.

The first step is not to fix the data. It is to agree on whether you trust it enough to act.

DAY 2

Clear Ownership and Accountability

In many organizations, data problems are endlessly discussed, yet responsibility and accountability remain strangely elusive. Meetings circle around symptoms like inconsistent numbers, late reports, and unclear metrics, while the underlying question is quietly avoided: "Who is actually accountable for this data?"

Ownership is uncomfortable because it forces prioritization. It requires someone to say, "This data matters enough that I am willing to stand behind it, make trade-offs, and accept scrutiny when things go wrong." Without that clarity, organizations drift into a familiar pattern: teams and people delay decisions, escalate issues sideways, and accountability becomes a shared abstraction rather than a concrete role.

This day exists to surface that discomfort. Not to assign blame, but to make visible a foundational truth: data that drives decisions cannot be ownerless.

From the 30 Days of Data Governance Posts

Yesterday, we talked about why data governance matters and what it is. Today, let's dig into one of the most powerful levers for trustworthy data: clear ownership and accountability.

Without clarity on who owns which data, errors and inconsistencies creep in. Imagine everyone in the office assuming someone else is responsible for cleaning, updating, or approving data, and chaos ensues. Processes break, decisions falter, and confidence in your organization's insights drops.

Good data governance fixes this by assigning **data owners and stewards**:

- **Owners** are accountable for the data's quality, completeness, and correctness.
- **Stewards** ensure day-to-day handling follows agreed rules and standards.

When responsibility is clear, everyone knows who to go to for answers, and decisions can be made with confidence and speed.

Over this series, we'll explore more practical ways to implement clear accountability, including:

- Identifying data owners for each critical data(set).
- Creating visible accountability structures.
- Using simple dashboards to track progress and compliance (Note: Dashboards can be useful, but are not resolving ownership troubles...).

Remember, trustworthy data comes from clear ownership. No owner, no accountability, no trust.

Looking Back From Practice

Ownership is often misunderstood as control.

In reality, it is closer to care.

Strong data owners are not the ones who touch the data most often. They are the ones who ensure decisions can be made without hesitation; that teams get an answer to their escalations, that conflicts get resolved rather than deferred, and that someone is willing to say “This is the number we stand behind” when the room is full and the pressure is high.

Where ownership is missing, something else fills the gap. Usually, the answer is a person, someone who has become the informal single point of truth through years of institutional memory and quiet dedication. I have met this person in almost every organization I have worked with. They are rarely the most senior. They are almost never formally recognized. And when they leave, the organization discovers just how much was held together by one individual rather than by structure. That is not a tribute to their skill. It reflects a system that never made ownership explicit.

I have watched this dynamic play out across financial services, retail, logistics, and technology organizations. The cost is rarely just technical. It is motivational. People lose confidence not only in the data, but in the system that is supposed to govern it, and that loss of confidence tends to spread.

Example: *A financial services firm struggled with conflicting revenue figures between Sales and Finance when they contacted me. Each department had its own extract, transformation logic, and timing assumptions. The breakthrough came when they appointed a Commercial Data Owner who owned the "revenue" definition across both teams. This person did not control the systems - they controlled the decision rights. When conflicts arose, they had the mandate to decide which methodology applied for which purpose. Within a quarter, revenue discussions shifted from "Whose number is right?" to "What do the numbers tell us?" That shift saved approximately 40 hours per month in reconciliation meetings.*

Ownership does not eliminate problems. It makes them visible, discussable, and solvable. That is where governance starts to move from theory into lived practice. And it is also where something else starts to shift: the people who were previously absorbing the friction quietly - reconciling, double-checking, compensating - finally have somewhere to take the problem. That change alone, in my experience, does as much for morale as it does for data quality.

DAY 3

Data Quality Is Queen

Clear ownership sets the foundation, but ownership alone cannot guarantee that data supports decisions. Even with the right people accountable, poor-quality data derails outcomes.

Data quality is one of those topics everyone agrees is important until it becomes inconvenient. Quality issues tend to surface under pressure: at month-end, before a board meeting, or when numbers suddenly do not align.

Quality is rarely experienced as a metric in itself. It is experienced as friction. As the need to double-check. As hesitation before sharing a report. As a quiet loss of confidence that something, somewhere, might be off. That is unfortunate, because data quality is a discipline worth developing real capability for.

This day exists to reframe data quality away from abstract dimensions and toward its real impact on trust and decision-making.

From the 30 Days of Data Governance Posts

After delving into clear ownership and accountability, let's focus today on **data quality**, the backbone of trusted insights.

Even with the right owners, poor-quality data can derail decisions. Think of it like a car with a full tank but flat tires: you have potential, but you cannot move forward effectively.

Good data quality means your data is:

- **Accurate**: Reflects reality.
- **Complete**: Nothing critical is missing.
- **Consistent**: The same information is the same everywhere.
- **Timely**: Available when needed.

Yes, some may want to add other quality dimensions, but honestly, start with a few, make some impact, and then expand. You will never be able to set an action plan if trying to follow 15 dimensions... right?

Implementing quality checks, validation rules, and regular audits ensures your data is
reliable, actionable, and decision-ready.

Over this series, we will look at ways to improve quality:

- Establishing simple metrics to monitor quality.
- Running regular audits and corrections.

- Automating validation where possible to reduce human error.

Remember: *high-quality data makes your decisions faster, smarter, and less stressful.* No quality, no trust, no confident decisions.

Looking Back From Practice

What matters most about data quality is not perfection, but predictability.

People can work with data that has known limitations. What breaks trust is inconsistency - when the same question yields different answers depending on timing, source, or who you ask. That inconsistency does something specific: it makes people doubt the next number before they have even looked at it. Once that habit sets in, it is hard to reverse.

I have been in organizations where the analysts spent the first hour of every morning cross-checking three systems before they felt safe enough to send anything to a manager. Not because the data was always wrong, but because it had been wrong often enough that no one trusted it without checking. That hour, multiplied across a team and over months, is a significant cost. And it never appeared on any budget line.

Many organizations get stuck trying to define every possible quality dimension upfront. In reality, progress comes from focus.

Choosing a small number of critical dimensions, applying them consistently, and making quality visible where it matters most. And be ready to act upon the results you see, not just measure them.

I have worked with organizations that had objectively imperfect data but still made excellent decisions, because everyone understood the limitations and worked within them. And I have seen organizations with technically clean data paralyzed by mistrust because that trust had never been deliberately built.

The condition of the data matters less than the shared understanding of it.

Example: *A healthcare provider was drowning in data quality initiatives: 15 different metrics, monthly reports no one read, and quality scores that did not reflect whether doctors could actually use the data. Through reviews and analysis, they reset by asking one single question: "Can a clinician trust this patient record enough to make a treatment decision?" They began focusing on three measures: record completeness for active patients, accuracy of medication lists, and timeliness of lab results. Within six months, clinician confidence in the system rose from 34% to 78%, measured through quarterly surveys. The key was not more metrics, it was metrics that mattered.*

High-quality data reduces defensive behavior. It allows teams to spend less energy validating inputs and more energy discussing outcomes. This changes not just how decisions are made, but how confident people feel making them. I have also noticed that quality improvements tend to shift the conversation within teams before they make any visible changes to leadership. The analyst who stops prefacing every report with a disclaimer. The manager who no longer asks “Are we sure about this?” before every decision. The meeting that ends on time because nobody needed to verify the inputs. These are not dramatic moments. They are quiet ones. But they accumulate and gradually reshape a team’s culture in ways no governance policy ever could. And that confidence earned through consistency rather than declared through policy is what governance is ultimately trying to build.

Day 4

Data Flows and Processes

Quality data sitting in isolated systems provides limited value. To support decisions, data must move through the organization reliably. Even when data is accurate and owned, it can still fail to support the business if it does not move in step with how work actually happens. Delays, hand-offs, and unclear transitions quietly undermine trust.

Data flow problems rarely announce themselves as such. They appear as late reports, repeated questions, or last-minute corrections. Teams feel the symptoms long before they see the cause.

This day exists to make those invisible flows visible and to show why governance must pay attention not just to data, but to how it travels and where it may be transformed.

From the 30 Days of Data Governance Posts

Now that you have your eyes on your data quality, it is time to explore how data flows through your organization, and why clear, well-designed processes are essential for making confident, timely decisions.

Even the best data can lose its value if it is stuck, delayed, or mismanaged. Think of your data like water: if it cannot flow where it is needed, your organization cannot operate at full capacity.

Why flow and processes matter:

- Unclear or blocked flows create errors, delays, and frustration.
- Teams spend time searching for data instead of using it.
- Decisions are delayed or made with incomplete information.

Key practices for mapping data flows:

- *Map critical data paths* to understand where data comes from, where it goes, and who touches it.
- *Streamline processes* to reduce hand-offs, bottlenecks, and delays.
- *Identify opportunities for automation and standardization* (Note: this is bullet #3 for a reason. Do bullets #1 and #2 first. Even for a part of your business. And THEN go for this one).
- *Use information architecture* diagrams to visualize flows, responsibilities, and dependencies. Seeing the big picture helps teams act faster and with confidence.

Smooth and transparent data flow is the lifeblood of trusted insights.
No flow, no insight, no impact.

Looking Back From Practice

Flow problems rarely begin as one obvious failure. More often, they build gradually through small delays, informal fixes, and historical decisions that once made sense but no longer match how the organization operates.

In facilitating flow-mapping sessions, I have found that the most useful moment is not when the diagram becomes accurate, but when someone points at the whiteboard and says, "That is not how it works." A rough sketch of a process, even if it is incomplete, slightly messy, and still being corrected as it is drawn, can surface more truth than a polished process document ever does. It gives people something concrete to challenge, and that is usually when the real conversation begins.

That is what makes mapping valuable. The goal is not a perfect diagram. It is shared visibility. Once people can see how data actually moves, the discussion changes. Teams stop defending their own part of the process in isolation and start seeing the cost of the whole path. That is usually the most lasting outcome of the exercise, and the one that is hardest to achieve through any other means.

Example: *A manufacturing company could not understand why its inventory reports were always three to five days behind reality. The data flowed through seven systems and twelve manual hand-offs. When they mapped the actual process, they discovered that two steps, data extraction from the warehouse management system and email-based approval from the supply chain manager, accounted for nearly 80% of the delay. They eliminated the email step by giving the system automatic approval rights for routine updates and moved the extraction to real-time API calls. Reporting latency dropped from 72 hours to 4 hours. The solution was not sophisticated; it was visible. Mapping revealed what everyone had assumed was working but was not.*

What tends to emerge over time for me, though, is that this kind of clarity does not last on its own. Systems change. New hand-offs accumulate. People inherit processes without inheriting the reasoning behind them. A flow map that was accurate in January can quietly stop reflecting reality by September, and the organization rarely notices until the latency creeps back or a question arises that no one can answer.

Governance of data flows is not a one-off mapping exercise. It is the discipline of returning to the process periodically and asking whether it still reflects how work actually happens. That does not always require a room full of people or a formal review. But it does require someone noticing that the process has changed, and taking responsibility for keeping the picture current.

That is what separates organizations that maintain flow clarity from those that rediscover the same problem every eighteen months. Not the quality of the original mapping, but the habit of tending it.

Day 5

The Cost of Bad Data

With ownership clarified, quality understood, and flows mapped, it becomes easier to recognize what happens when these elements are missing and what that absence actually costs.

The cost of bad data is often discussed in terms of lost revenue, regulatory fines, and inefficiencies. But the most damaging costs are harder to quantify.

Bad data teaches people and organizations a damaging reflex: verify before acting, question before deciding, delay before committing. Over time, this shapes behavior and culture in subtle but powerful ways.

Meetings start later because numbers must be reconciled. Decisions are delayed until "someone checks the data again." People build personal spreadsheets to confirm what systems should already tell them.

Opportunities pass by unnoticed. The decision that might have been made today waits until next week. The initiative that could have moved forward pauses while the numbers are checked once more.

What begins as caution gradually becomes routine, and the organization loses momentum without always noticing it.

This day exists to surface those hidden costs: not just the errors bad data creates, but the decisions it prevents before they are ever recognized as lost. Recognition, not fear, is what changes behavior.

From the 30 Days of Data Governance Posts

After seeing the benefits of how smooth data flows and well-designed processes keep your insights actionable, let's look at what happens when data goes wrong and why strong data governance is your safety net.

Even a small data error can ripple through your organization:

- Decisions are delayed or misinformed.
- Teams waste hours chasing the "right" numbers.
- Trust in your systems erodes, affecting strategy and operations.

Think of it like building a house on shaky foundations. No matter how beautiful the design, cracks will appear.

Strong data governance sets clear roles, policies, and quality checks, ensuring your data is accurate, complete, and trusted, so your organization can act with confidence.

Looking Back From Practice

The most significant cost of bad data is not the error itself, but the behavior it triggers.

When confidence in the numbers fades, organizations slow down. Decisions require more validation. Accountability becomes blurred. People rely on intuition instead of insight, not because they prefer it, but because it feels safer than committing to a number no one can fully defend.

I have sat in enough post-incident reviews to know that the real story is rarely about the bad data point itself. It is about the months of hesitation that preceded it, and the months of rebuilding that followed. The financial cost is visible on a spreadsheet. The cost in lost momentum and weakened confidence is not, but it is usually the larger number.

There is a particular atmosphere inside those reviews that I have come to recognize. The room is calm. The timeline is reconstructed carefully, step by step. The reasoning at every stage is sound. And then someone asks the question no one has yet asked: "What did we not know?" And the silence that follows is where the real answer sits, not in the data that was wrong, but in the data that was never there to begin with. Not in the decision that failed, but in the months of small hesitations that preceded it, each one signaling that something was off, and none of them acted upon because no one owned the signal.

Example: *An e-commerce platform suffered a seemingly minor data error: its product recommendation engine began showing "out of stock" items to customers, reducing conversion rates by 11%. The technical fix took 90 minutes. The organizational cost was far higher. For the next nine months, the merchandising team insisted on manually reviewing all automated recommendations before they went live, adding up to 3 days to every campaign launch and reducing their ability to respond to trends. The error cost them €40,000 in lost revenue. The loss of trust cost them €400,000 in missed opportunities. Trust can collapse in a moment; rebuilding it takes time.*

Good governance does not eliminate all errors. It creates conditions where issues are visible, owned, and addressed without drama. That is often the first moment when organizations feel the real return on governance, not in dashboards, but in regained confidence. And once confidence begins to return, the effect is cumulative. Teams move faster. Decisions feel less risky. The organization stops looking over its shoulder and starts looking forward. That regained momentum is often the clearest sign that governance is working.

Your Turn

The five chapters in this part cover the foundation: why trust becomes fragile, what poor data actually costs, and why governance enters the room not as a strategic ambition but as a response to something that no longer works. The questions below are not a checklist. They are a way of locating yourself to see where the themes in this part connect to your organization.

1. Where does hesitation show up in your organization?
Think about the moments when data is double-checked before a meeting, when two numbers circulate for the same thing, or when a decision is delayed until the numbers are confirmed. Those moments are your starting point, not symptoms to manage away, but signals worth paying attention to.

2. What is the conversation your organization keeps having?

Most organizations have a recurring data debate - a report that gets questioned every month, a metric that Finance and Operations can never agree on, a definition that means different things depending on who is in the room. Name it. That recurring conversation is probably where governance needs to begin.

3. Is poor data treated as a data or a decision problem?

This distinction matters more than it sounds. If the answer is almost always "It's a data problem", data governance will be handed to a technical team and stay there. If people begin to see it as a decision problem, ownership becomes possible.

4. Who already knows where the bodies are buried?

In every organization, some people know which datasets are unreliable, which processes break down, and which workarounds have quietly become permanent. They are rarely the most senior people in the room. They are worth finding early.

You do not need perfect answers here. You need honest ones. The clearer you are about where trust is already under strain, the more useful the rest of this book will be.

You have named the problem. The next part shows you how to build the ground beneath it, so that trust stops being a hope and starts being a structure.

Part 2

Building a Strong Foundation

If the first part of this book explored why trust in data erodes, the next question is more practical: "How do organizations build the foundations that allow data governance to work consistently?"

Once the need for data governance (i.e., the "why") is understood, the next challenge is turning intent into something that actually holds.

This part exists because good governance does not emerge from ambition alone. It requires structure, but the *right* kind of structure. One that supports people rather than constrains them, that brings consistency without creating bureaucracy, and that reduces friction and uncertainty in how work actually gets done. Not rules for their own sake. Clarity.

Here, the focus shifts from *why* data governance matters to *how* it is designed. Design for usability, not for perfection.

Roles, standards, definitions, architecture, and metrics are introduced not as ideals to strive for, but as practical tools that help organizations stop debating basics and move forward. None of that is possible without trust in data. The foundations in Part 2 are designed to produce one thing: *the confidence to act* without second-guessing.

Over-engineering this step is a common trap. Many organizations lose momentum. Either the foundation becomes too heavy, or it stays too vague. Both lead to the same outcome: governance that exists on paper but not in day-to-day work.

The intent of this part is different. Start simple. Make responsibilities visible. Anchor structure in real decision paths. A strong foundation is not about completeness; it is about creating enough shared clarity that teams can move forward together without revisiting the basics at every turn. The question is no longer why governance matters, but what needs to be true for decisions to work without hesitation.

One of the most counterintuitive lessons in this part: the most important data governance role in an organization is rarely the one with "data" in the title.

Day 6

Roles and Responsibilities

The cost of poor data and the foundations of trust are now clear. With that understanding established, attention turns to structure and structure begins with people.

One question must be asked before any role is defined: Who gets to decide, and who is accountable when it is wrong? That question, asked honestly, reveals more about real governance gaps than any role matrix.

Once organizations acknowledge the importance of governance, many rush to define roles. Titles are assigned, responsibility matrices are created, and on paper, everything appears clear.

In many cases, confusion remains.

The problem is not a lack of structure, but misalignment with reality. Roles are defined without regard for how decisions are actually made, where influence sits, or how work flows under pressure. People are "accountable" for data they cannot truly influence, while others shape outcomes without formal responsibility. When responsibilities are defined without regard for real decision paths, informal influence, or existing workloads, they quickly become decorative.

This day exists to slow that rush. To recognize that roles only stabilize governance when they reflect lived decision paths. Otherwise, they end up symbolic: visible but ineffective.

From the 30 Days of Data Governance Posts

Last week, in Part 1 of our series, we explored *why* data governance matters. Now, in Part 2, we dive into *the practical work*: how to get your data working for you and build a strong foundation for trusted insights.

A key step in making your data reliable is defining who does what and why it matters:

- Identify key roles: **data owners, data stewards, and custodians**. Each with clear accountabilities.
- Encourage **data champions** within teams to keep momentum, advocate for quality, and drive adoption.

Without clarity, even the best processes and tools can fall short. We will shortly explore how to define ownership for critical datasets, map hand-offs, and empower data champions, so governance sticks and your organization can act confidently.

Remember: strong roles and responsibilities are the glue that hold your data governance framework together. Get this right, and everything else flows more smoothly.

Looking Back From Practice

The most common mistake with roles is treating them as static assignments rather than living responsibilities. Effective roles evolve with the organization. They reflect how decisions are made, where knowledge sits, and who has the mandate to resolve conflicts. When roles are too rigid, people work around them. When they are too vague, nothing sticks.

There is another trap I see just as often, and it is more subtle: defining governance roles as if the only people who matter are those with "data" in their job title. In practice, data governance works when it *connects* with the roles that already exist. The architect who designs the systems data flows through. The developer who builds the pipelines. The financial controller who signs off on the numbers. The operations manager who owns the process at the point where data is created. These people are already making consequential data decisions every day. Governance roles do not exist in a vacuum. They exist in an ecosystem, and they only work when that ecosystem is mapped and respected.

Example: *A retail company created an elaborate RACI matrix with forty-seven different data-related roles. Six months later, no one* *used it. The problem was not the framework. It was that roles were designed in isolation by a consultant who never spoke to the people doing the work, nor reflected on the existing decision-making structure. They reset by identifying the five decisions that mattered most: "Can we launch this new product?" "Is this BOM (Bill of Materials) data accurate?" "Should we prioritize this dataset for remediation over others?" "Who resolves a conflict when our customer data and our sales data disagree?" "Which source is authoritative when inventory counts differ across systems?" For each decision, they asked: "Who actually makes this call today?" They formalized those existing decision-makers as data owners. Suddenly, roles felt recognizable because they mapped decisions people were already making, not decisions someone had imagined they should make.*

What matters most is not how many roles you define, but whether people recognize themselves in them. Legitimacy is the real test. When someone looks at a role and thinks "That is what I actually do, and those are the decisions I actually make," governance becomes actionable. When they look at a role and see something that bears no connection to their daily work, governance remains abstract in practice, regardless of how well documented it is. The goal is not a complete role catalog. It is a set of responsibilities that feel real, connect to actual decisions, and that people are willing to stand behind under pressure.

The original post introduced the data champion as someone within a team who keeps momentum and advocates for quality. In most organizations, this person almost always already exists. They are the analyst everyone calls when a number looks wrong, the manager who maintains the informal source of truth. In Day 16, we return to this in the context of stewardship and explore what happens when that informal role is finally made official, given time, and given mandate. A role that people recognize as their own will outlast any number of perfectly documented ones that are quietly ignored.

Day 7

Policies and Standards

With roles defined and responsibilities clear, the next question emerges, "What rules should guide how those people work?"

Policies and standards often carry a bad reputation and considerable emotional weight. People associate them with restriction, compliance, bureaucracy, loss of autonomy, and documents that few people read. As a result, organizations either overproduce them, hoping coverage will create control, or avoid them altogether. Yet when they are missing, organizations pay the price in confusion and rework.

Both approaches fail. The tension lies in balance. Too little guidance creates fragmentation. Too much creates resistance.

This day exists to surface the real tension: organizations need consistency to operate at scale, but flexibility to respond to context. Governance must navigate that balance deliberately, not by accident.

From the 30 Days of Data Governance Posts

Yesterday we talked about *roles and responsibilities*: who does what when it comes to data. But even the clearest roles can't succeed if everyone is making up their own rules. That is where *policies and standards* come in.

Have you ever opened a shared folder and found ten different versions of the same file, all slightly renamed? Or compared two reports from different teams that just don't match? That is what happens when every team speaks its own "data dialect."

Policies and standards are the antidote.

They don't exist to slow things down; they exist to make sure everyone moves in the same direction. Think of them as the traffic rules of your data world: agreed signals, common lanes, predictable flows. When everyone follows them, collaboration becomes easier, and decisions can be trusted.

The beauty of good standards is that they create consistency without chaos. They cut down on duplicate effort, reduce misunderstandings, and give people confidence that what they see in the data is the same truth others see too. And when designed pragmatically, they are not dusty documents nobody reads; they are practical, usable guides that support everyday work.

Without roles and responsibilities, standards don't stick.

And without standards, roles can't deliver.

In the coming days, we will explore how to make this real: from clear data definitions to information architecture and simple health metrics that keep data on track.

Looking Back From Practice

When people follow it without noticing they are doing so, the standard is effective: guiding behavior and enabling collaboration without drawing attention to itself.

The true test of a standard is when it is never discussed.

The moment standards become the subject of discussion, something has usually already gone wrong. When a standard works, it resolves ambiguity before it surfaces; when it fails that function because it is too rigid, too vague, or too disconnected from how work actually happens, the ambiguity it was supposed to absorb resurfaces instead as debate, and people are forced to negotiate what should already have been settled.

The organizations that struggle most with standards are those that wrote them in isolation, far from the people they are meant to guide, or those that wrote them primarily for auditors rather than practitioners. A standard that protects the organization from scrutiny but confuses the people doing the actual work is, in practice, no standard at all. The real test of a standard is not whether it passes a compliance review. It is whether someone picks it up when they face an ambiguous decision and finds it useful.

Example: *A logistics company had a 127-page data standards document that no one read. Data quality kept declining. We replaced it with a one-page document called "Data Decision Framework" that answered three questions: "What does this data represent?" "Who can change it?" "What happens if it's wrong?" Every team could keep this on their desk. Instead of prescribing every field format and validation rule, the framework provided principles for making consistent decisions. With sustained effort, data consistency improved by 40% over seven months, not because people followed more rules, but because they understood the ones that mattered.*

Successful organizations treat standards as guardrails, not walls. I have reviewed standards documents that were genuinely impressive: comprehensive, logically structured, and clearly written. And then I have sat with the people who were supposed to follow them and asked a simple question: "When you received this, what did you do?" The honest answer, more often than not, was: "I read the first few pages and then put it somewhere." Not because of bad intentions. Because the document was written for the organization's defense, not for the practitioner's daily decision. Those are two very different purposes, and blending them is one of the most common ways governance efforts are spent without effect.

Strong organizations treat standards as shared agreements, not rules to enforce or instruments of control. They are written with the practitioner in mind, tested against real decisions, and updated when the organization moves on. Consistency does not mean uniformity. It means predictable interpretation. Shared principles applied thoughtfully, by people who actually understand why those principles exist. That distinction is what turns a policy document from paperwork into something practical people reach for rather than file away.

Day 8

Data Definitions and Glossary

Standards create consistency, but consistency requires clarity about what words actually mean. Without that, even perfectly followed standards produce misalignment.

Semantic misalignment is one of the fastest ways to undermine trust. When teams use the same words but mean different things, alignment becomes impossible, even when the data is technically correct. Teams can be technically aligned using the same systems and reports, yet still fundamentally disagree because words mean different things. “Product”, “region”, “active”, “owner” - terms appear shared, but are not.

Glossaries are often underestimated because their impact is subtle and feels intangible. Yet language shapes decisions.

This day exists to show why shared language is not cosmetic, but foundational, especially as organizations grow and complexity increases.

From the 30 Days of Data Governance Posts

Clear policies and standards keep everyone in the organization moving in the same direction, but even the best rules can fall short if teams interpret data differently. To help everyone align, creating a **data glossary** ensures key terms (think "customer," "revenue," or "order") are understood the same way across teams.

Small differences in interpretation may seem minor, but they can quickly lead to misaligned decisions, duplicated work, and unnecessary frustration. By agreeing on common definitions, teams can trust the numbers they see and collaborate more efficiently.

> *A glossary is not a silver bullet for all data challenges, and it won't fix poor processes, messy systems, or bad governance.*

Think of it as a practical tool to support strong data governance and help teams collaborate more effectively. But don't rush into buying a fancy tool or software before understanding what definitions matter most and involve the people who actually use the data.

Building a glossary is a *joint effort.* It works best when the right people come together to agree on definitions, resolve ambiguities, and document meanings in a way that teams can consistently follow. As this continues, it becomes a trusted reference point, helping everyone speak the same language, act with confidence, and make future improvements easier.

This alignment lays the groundwork for better reporting, clearer communication, and more confident decision-making.

Looking Back From Practice

The value of a glossary is not completeness,
but ***convergence****.*

When organizations aim to define everything, they stall. When they focus on the terms that drive decisions, progress accelerates. A good glossary reflects shared agreement, not theoretical precision.

The conversations that happen when building a glossary are often more valuable than the glossary itself. I have facilitated definition workshops where a room full of smart, experienced people discovered, sometimes with visible surprise, that they had been using the same word to mean entirely different things for years, not out of carelessness, but because no one had ever asked. Each term had inherited a definition from somewhere, applied it to their own context, and assumed everyone else was working from the same starting point. The moment of shared recognition in those rooms - "So, when you say revenue, you mean…" - is one of the most productive moments in governance work. Not because anything has been fixed yet, but because the real problem has finally been named.

I have seen organizations spend months, or even years, building comprehensive data dictionaries that sat untouched on a shared drive (or expensive tool), because they were built for completeness rather than relevance. And I have sat in rooms where a single agreed definition of "active customer" transformed how leadership meetings run, cutting 70 minutes of debate down to 10 minutes of alignment. The difference is always whether the glossary connects to the decisions people are actually trying to make, and how seriously the adoption has been pursued.

Example: *A telecommunications company had different definitions of "active subscriber" across its five departments. Marketing counted anyone who opened an email in the last 120 days. Billing counted anyone with a valid payment method on file. Network Operations counted anyone who used mobile data in the last 30 days. Finance used a completely different calculation for reporting, with the contractual definition based on active service agreements. Customer Success counted anyone who had contacted the support team in the past quarter. All departments were represented in the organization's leadership. Arguments in leadership meetings consumed hours. They resolved it by asking: "What decision do we need this term to support?" The answer was churn prediction and revenue forecasting. They agreed that "active subscriber" meant "billable customer with usage in the last 60 days." The other* *definitions remained valid for each team's purposes, but the leadership dashboard used a different one. Meetings that previously took 90 minutes dropped to 20 minutes because the first 70 minutes, arguing about definitions, disappeared.*

With continued use, a trusted glossary becomes a reference point that extends well beyond the original terms it was built around. Teams start using it to settle new ambiguities. New joiners use it to understand how the organization thinks. And when a disagreement surfaces, as they always do, the question becomes "What does the glossary say?" rather than "Whose interpretation is right?" That movement, from competing opinions to shared reference, is where the real value of a glossary lives.

That role as a shared reference point for discussion and learning is central to data governance. Not because the glossary is exhaustive, but because it is trusted. It reflects shared agreements about what matters.

Where definitions are missing, debate takes the place of decision. Where they are shared, discussions move forward faster and with less friction.

Day 9

Information Architecture

Roles, standards, and definitions establish clarity within boundaries. Architecture reveals how those boundaries connect.

As organizations grow, their data landscapes rarely evolve by design. They evolve by accumulation. New systems are introduced to solve immediate needs. Integrations are added incrementally. Legacy platforms remain "for now" because replacing them is risky or expensive. Over time, the organization accumulates a complex web of systems, data flows, and dependencies that few people fully understand.

In this environment, leaders and teams often make decisions based on partial views. A Finance team models a system migration and estimates six months of work; nobody really asks what else connects to the platform they plan to retire, because no map exists. Teams optimize within their own boundaries, unaware of downstream impacts. Changes that appear small locally can have disproportionate effects elsewhere: breaking reports, degrading quality, or introducing hidden risk.

Information architecture exists to address this blind spot. By making complexity visible and manageable.

This day exists because information architecture is often treated as a technical exercise when, in reality, it is a governance tool. Without a shared understanding of how data, systems, and processes connect, governance decisions are made in isolation and misalignment becomes inevitable.

From the 30 Days of Data Governance Posts

Teams are now speaking the same language and policies are in place, but how do all the pieces fit together? Information architecture provides the blueprint showing how data, systems, and processes interconnect across your organization.

Think of it like navigating a city without a map. Streets, intersections, and traffic signals exist, but without a clear view of how they link, travel becomes inefficient, mistakes happen, and detours are frequent. Similarly, without a clear data map, teams struggle to find, use, or trust information. And decisions take longer or risk being misaligned.

A strong information architecture helps you:

- Understand where key data lives and how it flows.
- Identify bottlenecks, redundancies, and risk points.
- Clarify how processes, systems, and teams are connected.
- Provide a solid foundation for analytics, automation, and strategic initiatives.

It also gives leadership and teams confidence in their ability to make informed decisions, act efficiently, and avoid costly mistakes.

When aligned with roles, standards, and your data glossary, a good information architecture ensures your previous efforts actually work together. Decisions become faster, duplicate work decreases, and confidence in your insights grows.

You don't need perfect diagrams from the start. Keep it simple, focus on what matters most, and iterate as your organization learns.

Clarity is the goal.

Looking Back From Practice

The greatest value of information architecture is not precision, but perspective.

Architecture diagrams are rarely complete or perfectly up to date. Yet even imperfect views can change conversations. They surface dependencies, reveal bottlenecks, and make trade-offs explicit.

Once these links become visible, architecture discussions change completely. In one workshop, we began mapping systems and data flows on a wall using sticky notes. The diagram quickly became messy, systems were added, arrows redrawn, assumptions challenged in real time, as people pushed back on what they saw. Yet as the picture grew, something shifted. People started noticing relationships they had never considered before: "If that system feeds this report, our change next quarter will affect finance as well." The diagram was far from perfect. But once the landscape became visible, teams stopped focusing solely on their own systems and began to see the wider consequences. That is the real power of architecture maps: they reveal connections that were previously invisible.

Example: *A financial institution I supported was planning to retire a 25-year-old mainframe system. The project team estimated six months and €2 million. When they finally mapped all the data dependencies, they discovered that forty-seven downstream systems relied on this mainframe, including 12 that no one even knew existed. Several were customer-facing applications. The head of one business unit said, "If we had turned it off as planned, we would have crashed online banking for at least three days." The mapping exercise cost €60,000 and delayed the project by four months. It also prevented a disaster that would have cost tens of millions in lost* *revenue and regulatory fines. Architecture is not about pretty diagrams - it is about preventing expensive surprises.*

When architecture is absent, decisions rely on memory and assumption. When it is present, even at a high level, responsibility becomes shared rather than fragmented. People begin to see how their choices affect others and adjust accordingly.

Over time, this shared perspective begins to reduce surprises. Changes are introduced with greater care. Governance becomes proactive rather than reactive, because complexity is no longer hidden. And perhaps more importantly,

---

People stop making decisions in isolation and start making them in context.

This, in a complex data landscape, is where most of the real risk is actually managed.

DAY 10

Simple Metrics and KPIs

With the structure in place (roles, standards, definitions, and architecture), the natural question becomes, "How do we know if it is working?"

Measurement is often where governance ambition collides with organizational reality. Faced with uncertainty, organizations tend to measure more. New metrics are added to track quality, compliance, adoption, and performance. Dashboards grow. Reports multiply. Visibility increases but clarity often does not.

Over time, metrics become noise. Teams struggle to distinguish signal from distraction. Measurement shifts from learning to justification, and governance becomes something to report on rather than improve.

This day exists to challenge a common misconception: that more measurement leads to better control. Restraint, however, is a data governance skill. Choosing what *not* to measure is as important as deciding what to track.

From the 30 Days of Data Governance Posts

You've defined roles, set standards, agreed on a data glossary, and mapped your information architecture. The next question is, "How do you know your data is actually healthy and trustworthy enough to track business KPIs?" That's where simple metrics and KPIs come in: practical tools to measure data quality and progress without overwhelming teams. Starting with data quality metrics is essential.

Start with your most critical datasets and focus on a handful of meaningful indicators: **completeness**, **accuracy**, **consistency**, and **timeliness**. Too many metrics can create noise, while a few well-chosen KPIs give clarity, highlight trends, reveal gaps, and show whether processes and standards are being followed. Once your data can be trusted, these metrics form the foundation for business KPIs, enabling teams and leadership to make confident, informed decisions.

Metrics are not meant to police teams or generate endless reports.

They are a mirror of your data's health, helping prioritize improvements, refine processes, and ensure your insights are reliable before tracking business performance. When aligned with roles, standards, glossary, and architecture, these simple KPIs create a powerful feedback loop, keeping data actionable and decisions sound.

Looking Back From Practice

The most effective governance metrics are those that create conversation, not compliance.

When metrics are too many, too abstract, or too detached from decisions, people disengage. They report numbers without reflecting on what they mean. Improvement stalls not because the data is wrong, but because nobody feels responsible for acting on it.

I have been in organizations with 50-metric data governance dashboards where no one could tell me which three numbers they would act on if they went red.

That is not measurement - it is decoration.

The volume of metrics creates an illusion of data governance maturity that masks the absence of any real accountability for the underlying data.

There is a quieter version of the same problem that I find just as damaging. When the data behind the metrics is itself unreliable, the dashboard becomes a confidence trick. Decision-makers see a green indicator and feel safe, unaware that the green is based on incomplete inputs, inconsistent definitions, or a process last validated two years ago. I have made a habit of asking, in any governance review: "Do we trust the data behind this metric?" This does not make me popular. The pause before the answer is usually instructive.

Example: *A media company had been tracking forty-six data quality metrics across all datasets for many years when I started advising them. Every month, a 25-page report went to leadership. No one read it, and the quality did not improve. They then created a dashboard for leadership engagement, but that made no difference either. They eventually replaced the entire framework with three metrics tied to actual pain points: "Can we publish tonight's edition without manual data fixes?" "Do advertising clients trust our audience numbers?" "Can analysts answer executive questions without re-checking source data?" They tracked these weekly with red/amber/green status. When a metric went red, they held a 15-minute problem-solving session, not a blame meeting. Within four months, manual fixes dropped by 60%, client* *complaints fell by 40%, and analyst confidence rose from 52% to 81%. The difference was not measurement. It was relevance.*

In contrast, a small set of well-chosen indicators can change behavior. When metrics are clearly linked to ownership and visible where decisions are made, they stop being a reporting obligation and become a feedback mechanism rather than judgment.

Teams use them to understand trends, adjust practices, and prevent issues before they escalate. Leadership uses them to make better decisions. That is when measurement starts to support maturity rather than merely document effort. And that is also when governance stops feeling like overhead, because the people doing the work can see, in simple terms, whether it is making a difference.

Metrics that matter do not just measure quality. They give people permission to stop checking and start deciding. That permission is confidence.

Your Turn

This part focused on building the foundations for everything that follows: roles that reflect real decision paths, standards that create consistency without bureaucracy, definitions that reduce endless negotiation of meaning, architecture that makes the invisible visible, and metrics that inform rather than overwhelm. The questions below are not a review. They are an invitation to test which of those ideas actually landed.

1. Do people recognize themselves in the roles you have defined?

This is the real test, not whether a RACI exists, but whether the people named in it would agree it reflects what they do. If the answer is mostly no or "I'm not sure", the structure is ahead of the organization. That is not a failure; it is information.

2. What is the one term your organization cannot agree on?
There is almost always one. Customer. Revenue. Active. Location. Lead time. Find it. That single term is often the source of more friction than any technical issue. Agreeing on one definition, even provisionally, even imperfectly, is a foundation worth building.

3. What is the one element of your foundation that, if clarified, would reduce the most friction in decisions right now?
It could be a role, a standard, a dependency, metrics, KPIs, or a compliance expectation that people are following without fully understanding. The point is not to fix everything at once. It is to identify what would make the next decision easier, clearer, or less contested.

4. What would change tomorrow if one person left?
If the answer is a lot, data governance is still held together by individuals instead of by structure. That is not unusual at this stage. But it is a useful tension to name: where does the organization depend on memory rather than process?

A strong foundation does not need to be complete. It needs to be honest. What you know, what you have in place, and where the gaps are, that clarity is more useful than a polished framework built on unexamined assumptions underneath it.

When these foundations hold, people stop asking "Can we trust this?" and start reflecting on "What does this tell us?" That shift is the first sign that confidence is forming.

PART 3

Avoiding Common Pitfalls

Even with good intentions and a solid setup, data governance can quietly drift off course.

This part exists to make the invisible visible.

The challenges explored here, from silos and manual workarounds to missing data, conflicting sources, and inconsistent processes, are rarely accidents. They are signals: indicators that data governance is unclear, misaligned, or no longer connected to how the organization actually operates. I have walked into organizations where every one of these was present at the same time, each treated as a separate problem and none recognized as part of the same pattern.

These pitfalls tend to share a common signature: things that were working quietly start requiring attention again. A metric that was once trusted is now questioned. A workaround reappears. A process that seemed settled has drifted. Each signal is small.

Together, they indicate that governance has lost contact with how the organization actually operates. Confidence declines and defensive behaviors arise.

Most organizations recognize these symptoms immediately. What is less obvious is that they are not isolated problems, but part of a broader pattern at play.

The value of this part is not in pointing out what goes wrong: most organizations already feel it. This part helps you recognize those signals early, understanding why they occur and seeing how governance can be used to prevent firefighting rather than institutionalize it.

This part is where the book gets uncomfortable. These are not theoretical risks. They are patterns that are almost already present in all organizations. The five chapters that follow answer one question directly: What breaks governance, even when the intent is right and the design is sound?

The goal is not perfection, but reliability over time.

Day 11

Data Silos

With the foundation in place, attention shifts to obstacles that quietly undermine governance. The first and often most persistent is fragmentation.

Data silos are rarely created deliberately. No organization sets out to fragment its information landscape. Instead, silos form gradually, through a series of rational decisions made under local pressure.

Teams are asked to deliver quickly. Systems are implemented to solve specific needs. Access is restricted "temporarily" to reduce risk or complexity. Each decision makes sense in isolation. Gradually, those decisions accumulate into separation.

What makes silos particularly difficult to address is that they often feel productive at first. Teams move faster when they control their own data. They avoid coordination overhead. They optimize locally. The problem only becomes visible when collaboration is required: when decisions span functions, markets, or time horizons.

This day exists to surface a critical insight: silos are not primarily a data architecture problem. They are an organizational design problem. They reflect how incentives, accountability, and trust are distributed across the organization.

Until that reality is acknowledged, technical integration alone will not resolve them.

From the 30 Days of Data Governance Posts

We wrapped up the foundations with metrics and KPIs. But even if you measure all the right things, what happens to your organization if each department keeps its own version of the truth? Welcome to *the world of data silos.*

> *Data governance never sleeps. It is always awake,*
> *making sure data flows where it should.*
> *The real question is, "Are you awake to the risks of silos?"*

Data silos occur when teams or systems hold onto their own datasets without sharing or aligning them. On the surface, this might look harmless. After all, marketing, finance, and operations all have different needs. But in practice, silos block collaboration, duplicate efforts, and create conflicting versions of reality. That's when trust starts to crumble and decisions suffer.

Silos are rarely just a technical problem. They form because of organizational structures, misaligned incentives, and a lack of trust. Breaking them down requires *leadership, communication, and a clear reason for people to work together.* Technology can support, but people and purpose drive the real change.

Think of it this way: if data is the bloodstream of your organization, silos are like clots. They stop value from flowing, slow down decision-making, and make it harder to see the big picture.

When silos persist, everyone loses. Teams spend more time debating whose numbers are "right" than acting on insights. Opportunities are missed, and the organization becomes reactive instead of proactive. When silos dissolve, collaboration improves, insights gain speed, and trust grows across the board.

Supporting organizations in overcoming silos means creating alignment on shared goals, building bridges between departments, and enabling collaboration without forcing everyone into the same mold.

When people, processes, and systems connect,
silos dissolve, and decisions get stronger.

Looking Back From Practice

Silos persist because they feel safe.

When shared data is unreliable or politically contested, teams protect what they control. They create their own definitions, their own extracts, their own logic. With time, this behavior becomes normalized and eventually defended.

I have been in rooms where a team lead said openly, "Of course, we keep our own data. The central warehouse has let us down three times in two years." Rational self-protection, not stubbornness. It also means that breaking silos requires more than access; it requires rebuilding the trust that was lost. Technical integration without that trust-building work tends to be resisted, worked around, or quietly ignored.

Example: *A multinational bank had fourteen different "customer risk score" calculations across divisions. Regulatory reporting used one, Lending used another, Wealth management used a third. When regulators questioned inconsistencies, the bank discovered that each division had created its own score because it did not trust the central data warehouse, which had failed them repeatedly in 2013 during a system migration. Five years later, the technical issues were resolved, but behaviors had not really changed. Breaking the silos required more than fixing systems. The Chief Data Officer spent four months rebuilding trust: showing data quality metrics publicly, holding "office hours" where people could challenge the central scores, and giving divisions the ability to flag concerns* *without penalty. Slowly, teams started using the shared score. The technical solution took three weeks. The trust-building took almost nine months. But only the second actually worked.*

Data governance changes are not about access first, but about confidence. When ownership is clear, definitions are shared, and quality is predictable, the perceived risk of sharing decreases.

Breaking silos is rarely about forcing alignment.
It is about creating conditions where alignment feels less risky than isolation.

This transformation takes time, and it only happens when governance deliberately addresses trust as much as it does structure.

Day 12

Manual Processes vs Automation

Silos fragment data across boundaries. Manual processes, by contrast, create friction within those boundaries.

Manual processes can begin as sensible compromises. A report is built overnight to fill a gap in the system. A manual sign-off is added because no one trusts the automated output. What starts as a practical fix can quietly become a structural dependency, one that is rarely questioned until it breaks. In the early stages, these solutions are not only acceptable; they are necessary.

Problems emerge when temporary fixes become permanent dependencies.

Over time, knowledge becomes tacit. Only a few people know which checks matter, which fields are optional, and which exceptions can be ignored. Automation is then proposed as a remedy, often under pressure to scale or standardize.

This day exists to challenge a deeply ingrained assumption: that automation is always a sign of maturity. In reality, automation amplifies whatever process it replaces, clarity or confusion.

From the 30 Days of Data Governance Posts

After tackling silos, let's look at another challenge: **manual processes**. Spreadsheets, emails, and copy-paste solutions are often where organizations begin. They feel flexible and "good enough", until they become bottlenecks. Hours get lost reconciling versions, updates slip through the cracks, and trust in the numbers starts to erode. Sound familiar from those siloed setups?

Automation sounds like the perfect answer: faster, consistent, and less prone to error. And it can be transformative, when done right. But here is the tricky part: automating a messy or unclear process doesn't fix the problem; it just makes the chaos run faster.

Automating data you don't trust only spreads inaccuracies further and faster.

So, what's the right approach?

Use manual checks where human judgment, context, and nuance are required. Automate repetitive, rules-based tasks where efficiency and accuracy matter most.

Build confidence step by step: as your processes stabilize, let automation take over gradually.

Strong governance ties it all together. It ensures you know which processes belong to people, which ones can be handled by machines, and how to connect both in a way that supports your business goals. Automation is not about replacing people: it is about freeing them from firefighting so they can focus on insight, strategy, and value.

Looking Back From Practice

The question is not *whether* to automate, but *what* to automate. And more importantly, when.

Manual processes are often the right answer at the time. They emerge where understanding is still incomplete, where systems are not yet aligned, or where coordination needs a human layer to hold things together.

What looks inefficient later often began as the only way to move forward with confidence. The challenge is not their existence, but how long they remain unquestioned once the context has changed. The issue is not that they exist. It is that they rarely get revisited once they are working well enough.

I have repeatedly noticed a pattern in how automation conversations tend to start. Someone senior, usually under pressure to reduce costs or improve speed, asks why a particular process still requires so many people. A consultant or an internal team produces a slide showing how automation could cut the effort by 60%. The business case looks compelling. The decision is made. And nobody in that room has asked the most important question, “Do we actually understand this process well enough to codify it?”

Example: *An insurance company I worked with automated its claims validation process to reduce manual review time. Sounded fair at first. They spent €800,000 building the system. Three months after launch, manual review time had actually increased by 30%. Why? The automation had codified seven years of accumulated workarounds and undocumented exceptions. Claims processors were now spending their time investigating why the automated system flagged legitimate claims as suspicious. They had to reverse-engineer the automation logic to understand what it was checking. The company eventually spent another €500,000 and six months redesigning the process properly, defining clear validation rules, documenting legitimate exceptions, and removing outdated checks. Only then did automation deliver value.*

What that example illustrates is not a technology failure. The technology did exactly what it was asked to do. The failure was that nobody had done the data governance work first: clarifying which rules were real, which exceptions were legitimate, and which workarounds had outlived their purpose. Once you automate a process, all of those hidden decisions become invisible. They stop being questioned. They run at scale, silently, until something breaks badly enough that someone traces the logic back to its source.

Strong organizations approach automation with restraint. They stabilize processes first. They make variation explicit and decide deliberately which variation matters and which is noise. They ask, "If we remove the human judgment from this step, what are we removing?" Governance provides the criteria for that question.

When automation follows clarity, it frees people from correction work and lets them focus on the decisions that genuinely require human judgment. When it precedes clarity, it compounds the problem and makes it significantly harder to resolve.

And remember, you cannot automate stupid.

DAY 13

Missing Data and Gaps

Flawed processes create visible problems. Missing data, by contrast, creates invisible ones, and invisible problems are often the most dangerous.

Missing data is one of the most serious forms of data failure, precisely because it goes unnoticed. Reports can look complete. Dashboards can show healthy trends. Decisions can feel well informed until an assumption is challenged or a consequence materializes. Stakeholders may call this "poor data quality," even though the data was never there.

Gaps rarely result from neglect. They emerge from optional fields, undefined ownership, unclear processes, or silent assumptions about what “doesn’t matter.” Eventually, these gaps become normalized. People stop asking whether the data is complete and start working around its absence.

This day exists to highlight a subtle but critical risk: incomplete data does not slow decisions. It distorts them. By the time the gap becomes visible, the decision has already been shaped by that risk.

From the 30 Days of Data Governance Posts

Even with roles, standards, a glossary, and clear processes in place, missing data and gaps can quietly sabotage your insights. A report may look complete, but hidden gaps, like skipped fields, incomplete records, or untracked transactions, can distort the story your data is telling. That is why identifying blind spots early is crucial: you can't act on what you can't see. Think of it like a puzzle: missing pieces leave holes in the picture, and drawing conclusions from incomplete information risks costly mistakes. Detecting gaps is not about blame: it is about clarity. By understanding where data is missing, why it is missing, and how it flows across systems, teams can address root causes rather than just symptoms.

Key steps to tackle missing data and gaps:

- Track which datasets are incomplete or inconsistent.
- Investigate the reasons behind missing or delayed data.
- Ensure that processes, roles, and systems support completeness.
- Prioritize remediation where it impacts critical decisions.

A strong governance framework ties it all together: clear ownership, agreed standards, and well-defined processes make gaps easier to spot, fix, and prevent. When teams know which sources are reliable and where the holes are, confidence in the numbers grows, and decisions are more informed.

Looking Back From Practice

> *The most damaging effect of missing data is false confidence.*

When gaps are unknown, decisions feel solid and justified, until they fail. The cause is then hard to trace, because the analysis was often correct given what was available. The reasoning held. The conclusion followed logically from the inputs. The inputs were incomplete in a way no one had thought to question. Data governance introduces discipline by making absence visible, making ownership explicit, and asking uncomfortable questions: what are we not seeing, and why?

Reviews involving missing data have a specific texture. When the cause is wrong data, there is usually a traceable error: a system failure, a transformation mistake, or a manual input gone wrong. When the data never existed to begin with, there is often nothing to point at. The analysis was done well. The decision was made carefully. The data field that would have changed everything simply was not there, and no one had ever added it to the completeness checklist because no one had anticipated needing it. I have sat in those rooms more times than I would like. The silence after "the data was never collected" lands differently from any other kind of governance failure. There is no one to blame. There is only a gap that nobody owns.

Example*: A retail chain was expanding rapidly and used a "revenue per store" metric to decide which locations to replicate. During a broader review I was doing, this metric showed strong performance in suburban locations. They opened 23 new suburban stores at a cost of €47 million. Eighteen months later, 19 of those stores were underperforming. What went wrong? The "revenue per store" calculation was missing online sales attributed to each location: the original successful stores had high foot traffic and high online pickup rates. The new stores only replicated the foot traffic, not the online integration. The data was not wrong in itself; it was incomplete. The gap cost them €31 million in write-downs and lease obligations. One missing data field, "online revenue attributed to store", was the difference between success and failure.*

By defining completeness and giving it an owner, organizations shift from reactive correction to proactive understanding. In mature organizations, completeness is treated not as a technical metric but as a decision requirement. People know which data must be present before action is taken and who is accountable when it is not. That discipline gradually changes the governance conversation from “How do we fix it?” to “What do we need to know before we act?”

Day 14

Conflicting Sources

Missing data creates blind spots. Conflicting data, by contrast, creates gridlock.

Few things break trust faster than conflicting numbers. In those moments, two reports produce different answers to the same question, and data stops being an asset and becomes a liability. Meetings grind to a halt. Credibility wears down. Decisions are deferred or made on instinct rather than evidence.

Conflicting sources are rarely accidental. They reflect historical decisions, parallel system development, unresolved ownership, and local optimization. Over time, these inconsistencies become embedded and politically sensitive.

When two numbers compete, governance begins by choosing one version to stand behind, and making that choice visible.

This day exists to bring a difficult reality into focus: "one version of the truth" is not a technical goal. It is a data governance decision and governance decisions require someone with the authority to make them.

From the 30 Days of Data Governance Posts

You've addressed the silos, stabilized processes, and filled in data gaps. But what happens when two systems tell different stories? Conflicting sources are like competing voices in a meeting: without alignment, decisions stall, mistakes creep in, and trust in your data wavers.

These conflicts often arise from legacy systems, inconsistent calculations, or differences in data entry practices. Left unchecked, they can silently distort your insights. Spotting and resolving discrepancies early not only restore trust but also keep your data reliable. How to tackle conflicting sources:

- Identify discrepancies across systems and reports.
- Prioritize conflicts that affect critical decisions.
- Standardize definitions, calculations, and processes.
- Align stakeholders on *one clear source of truth.*

Remember: Data Governance keeps it simple: clear roles, standards, and agreed processes make resolving conflicts straightforward and prevent new ones.

Looking Back From Practice

The real cost of conflicting sources is not disagreement.

It is paralysis.

When no source is trusted, organizations slow down. People bring their own numbers to defend their position. Decisions are deferred or made on instinct. What should be analysis becomes negotiation. And by the time the negotiation ends, the energy for the actual decision has often left the room.

There is a particular version of this that I find hardest to watch, and it has nothing to do with the numbers themselves. It is what happens to the people in those meetings as this continues. In the early months, the reconciliation feels frustrating but manageable. By the sixth or twelfth month, it has become the culture. People arrive already defensive, already expecting to spend the first half of any meeting establishing a shared baseline rather than working from one. They stop expecting the data to be reliable. They start managing around it. And at some point, without anyone announcing it, the organization quietly stopped being data-driven because it found the data could not be relied on to drive anything.

The worst version is when it happens in front of external stakeholders. At this point, the cost is not just time. It is credibility.

Example: *A software company's board meeting imploded when the CFO reported €3.2M in Q3 revenue, whilst the CRO reported €4.1M* *for the same quarter. Both were actually "correct" according to their systems. Finance counted revenue when invoices were paid. Sales counted it when contracts were signed. Neither was wrong; they were measuring different things. For two months, every executive meeting began with their "40 minutes of reconciliation". They finally resolved it by creating a "Revenue Council" - the CFO, CRO, and Revenue Operations lead - who met every month to pre-align numbers and document their methodology. They agreed that management reporting would use "recognized revenue" (Finance's method), whilst Sales would track "booked revenue" (their method) for compensation purposes. Both metrics remained, but everyone understood which one applied to which decision. The reconciliation meetings disappeared.*

Strong data governance restores momentum by making trade-offs explicit. It defines which source is authoritative, for which purpose, and under which conditions. That clarity reduces debate. People no longer need to defend their version of the truth; they can work from a shared starting point. Once that starting point is shared, energy can move away from reconciliation and back to decision-making.

DAY 15

Inconsistent Processes

Process consistency is frequently misunderstood and is often the deeper cause of the conflicting data that Day 14 addressed.

The goal is not for every team to do things the same way. It is to make sure the decisions produced by those processes can be compared reliably. These are different targets, and mixing them is one of the most common governance mistakes. Standardizing how a form is filled out, or how a call is logged, or how a region calculates its weekly close. They are only worth doing if the lack of consistency is creating a comparison problem that matters to someone making a real decision. Uniformity for its own sake breeds resistance. Comparability, tied to a specific decision, earns cooperation. The question to ask is never "Is everyone doing this the same way?" but rather "If two teams produce results from this process and we put them side by side, can we trust what we are comparing?"

When organizations lose that comparability, the root cause is often process inconsistency.

These inconsistencies rarely begin as problems. They usually emerge from good intentions, perhaps better described as process variations. A workaround saves time. A local adjustment helps meet a deadline. A shortcut removes friction.

Individually, these variations seem harmless. Collectively, they make comparisons unreliable and confidence harder to sustain. They fragment how data is created, handled, and interpreted.

As inconsistencies become the norm, comparability disappears. The same data element can take on different meanings depending on who created it, when, and how. Decisions that rely on comparison across units, periods, or regions become unreliable.

This day exists to reframe why consistency matters: not as a form of control, but as the condition that allows organizations to compare, learn, and act with confidence.

From the 30 Days of Data Governance Posts

You've heard it before: the "Just do it this way, it's faster" or "We've always done it this way" in one team, or a quick shortcut there. But before long, you have multiple versions of the same process co-existing. Each one is slightly different. Each one produces slightly different results. The outcome? Confusion, rework, compliance risks, and leaders who can't trust the numbers put in front of them.

That is why process consistency is as critical as data quality itself.

Even the cleanest, most accurate data will lose value if it flows through inconsistent methods. Two teams working on the same dataset can deliver two very different answers simply because their ways of working don't align.

Consistency doesn't mean bureaucracy for the sake of control. It means creating reliability, trust, and comparability across your organization's decisions. It ensures that insights are not just "right once" but right every time, no matter who is involved.

Looking Back From Practice

Consistency does not mean rigidity. The strongest organizations standardize where outcomes must be comparable and allow flexibility where context demands it. Data governance matters because it creates discipline between standardization and flexibility, and that distinction is more important than most organizations realize. The pattern is easy to miss until aggregation exposes it: two teams using the same template, each applying a slightly different definition. Nothing looks wrong locally. The problem only appears when the numbers are combined and suddenly, what looked consistent reveals itself as incomparable.

In my experience, one of the quickest ways to trigger resistance to governance is to standardize without explaining why. People reasonably ask why a field must be captured in a specific format or why a step must be performed in a particular way. When the answer is simply "Because the policy says so," adoption collapses. When the answer is "Because without it, we cannot compare results across regions and make the right investment decision," people understand and the discussion changes. The discipline is not in enforcing uniformity. It is important to be clear about which variation matters and why.

What I find most instructive is rarely the visible failure itself. It is the underlying pattern that has been there for years: inconsistency that has been undermining comparability long before anyone notices it. Regional teams run slightly different processes. Month-end cut-offs are applied differently depending on who is doing the close. Categorization rules evolve locally and are never reconciled centrally. Each variation seems harmless and manageable in isolation. Together, they create data that looks complete but does not mean the same thing, and leadership ends up making decisions based on aggregated numbers that were never truly comparable in the first place.

Example: *A pharmaceutical company had eight regional teams running clinical trials. Each team had evolved its own process for "patient eligibility verification." Some used automated checks,* *others manual review. Some were verified at screening, others at enrollment. During the audit, the regulator found that 23% of enrolled patients across all regions would not have qualified under a consistent standard. The company was not fined because it was caught during an internal audit, but it had to re-verify 4,400 patient records and delay two trials by five months at a cost of €18 million. The root cause was not bad data; it was eight different interpretations of the same protocol. They redesigned the verification process with non-negotiable steps (automated eligibility checks using specific criteria) and flexible steps (how teams communicated with sites). Within six months, verification consistency rose from 77% to 98%. The lesson was not "Eliminate all variation," it was "Know which variation matters."*

When processes align in the places that matter most, data becomes dependable across boundaries. When they do not, even high-quality data loses value the moment it is aggregated, compared, or used beyond its local context. Over time, process consistency reduces rework, strengthens confidence in shared numbers, and supports decisions that must scale beyond local optimization.

Consistency, in this sense, is not about control. It is about creating the conditions where people can stop verifying and start deciding; where trust in the process becomes confidence in the outcomes.

Your Turn

Silos. Manual workarounds. Missing data. Conflicting sources. Inconsistent processes. These are not exotic problems. They are the ordinary texture of how data governance drifts in practice: slowly, sensibly, and often for entirely rational reasons. The questions below are worth sitting with, whether or not you read this part in sequence.

1. Which silo in your organization is least visible to leadership?

The ones leadership knows about are already being managed, at least nominally. The dangerous silos are the ones that have been normalized, where each team has settled into the assumption that sharing is not really expected, and where no one escalates because the workaround has become the process.

2. Where has a temporary fix become a permanent dependency?

Most organizations have at least one. Something that was never meant to last but never got removed. Something everyone uses but no one owns. Something that works just well enough that it is never questioned. These are not failures. They are evidence that the official process stopped fitting reality at some point.

3. What does your organization not know that it does not know?

Missing data is dangerous precisely because it is invisible. The question is not just what data is absent, but which decisions are being made as if that absence does not matter. That missing field may be the difference between a good decision and an expensive one.

4. Where does process inconsistency cost the most?

Not all variation matters equally. Where does inconsistency make outcomes incomparable across regions, teams, time periods, or systems? That is where standardization earns its keep. Everywhere else, flexibility is probably fine.

Avoiding those pitfalls does not make data governance perfect. It makes it reliable enough to move forward without constant doubt. Reliability is what confidence is built from. These pitfalls are worth naming without drama. The goal is not to list everything that is broken. It is to identify one or two patterns that, if addressed, would reduce the most friction. Start there.

Part 4

Embedding Governance in Daily Work

Data governance only creates value when it is lived, not just documented.

This part exists because frameworks alone do not change behavior. What changes behavior is responsibility that feels real, feedback that is visible, and practices that fit into how people already work. The difference between this part and the ones before it is the difference between design and reality, between what governance says should happen and what actually happens when people are under pressure, working to a deadline, and making dozens of small data decisions every day.

Here, governance moves off the page and into daily routines. Stewardship, validation, reporting, communication, and learning become the mechanisms through which trust is built consistently rather than occasionally. This is where ownership becomes practical, quality becomes observable, and governance starts to hold under real conditions.

This is the turning point. When governance is embedded, it stops feeling like extra work and starts becoming the way work gets done. Data issues are addressed earlier. Conversations become clearer. Escalations become less dramatic.

This part is about making that shift real: the point where governance stops being a design exercise and becomes a daily practice, owned by the people doing the work, visible in the decisions they make, and sustained by the routines they build around it. When the previous part showed what breaks data governance, this one shows what makes it hold. Not in a policy, but in practice. In the behaviors, routines, and responsibilities that make governance part of day-to-day work.

This is the point where governance becomes part of how the organization operates.

Day 16

Data Stewardship

Understanding governance is not enough. Responsibility must translate into daily action, and this is where stewardship becomes essential.

By this point in the journey, most organizations intellectually understand governance. They can explain why it matters, where things go wrong, and what should be in place. And yet, something still feels fragile.

The reason is simple: understanding does not change behavior. Responsibility does.

This is often where organizations struggle to turn good intentions into consistent good practices. The framework exists. Roles are named. Expectations are documented. People might even be identified. But day-to-day decisions still rely on individual judgment, personal workarounds, and quiet heroics. Issues are fixed just enough to move on, without being resolved in a way that prevents recurrence.

Data stewardship is where governance stops being conceptual and becomes operational. It is the moment when someone is expected to care not just in theory, but in day-to-day work: to notice when something is off, to follow up, and to close the loop.

This day exists to surface a reality many organizations underestimate:

Data governance rarely fails because policies are missing. It fails because no one feels responsible for applying them consistently under pressure.

When deadlines tighten and priorities collide, policies become suggestions unless someone feels accountable for upholding them. This is where policies meet pressure, and either hold or break.

From the 30 Days of Data Governance Posts

Reaching Part 4 of the series, let's focus on *embedding governance into daily work.*

You can have the clearest policies and frameworks, but without someone actively taking care of the data every day, governance stays on paper. **Data stewardship is about real responsibility**:

making sure definitions are applied, quality checks are performed, and issues are actually fixed.

A good steward isn't just a name on a chart. They:

- Know exactly which data they are responsible for.
- Monitor, correct, and maintain data quality.
- Bridge the business and IT so everyone speaks the same language.
- And yes, they are probably already in place in your organization; you just need to make it a bit more official and clearer.

When stewardship is practical, governance stops being abstract and becomes part of everyday work.

It is the link between strategy and action, the thing that ensures trusted data flows through your organization, not just policies on paper.

Looking Back From Practice

Stewardship works when it feels legitimate.

In many organizations, stewards already exist informally. They are the people others turn to when numbers do not make sense or when definitions are unclear. Making stewardship explicit does not create new responsibility; it acknowledges what is existing and gives it a mandate. That distinction matters enormously. When you formalize someone who was already doing the work, they gain authority without losing credibility. When you appoint someone to a stewardship role who has no prior connection to the data, you create a title without a relationship, and titles without relationships do not change behavior.

One recurring issue that trips organizations up: they design stewardship by copying a model from a conference or a consultant's deck, without asking whether it fits their structure, culture, or scale. A stewardship model that works in a global bank will not automatically work in a mid-sized logistics firm, and the reverse is equally true. The roles, the cadence, the escalation paths, the time allocation - all of these need to be calibrated to the organization as it actually is, not as a framework imagines it should be. Keep what works, leave the rest.

It is also worth being precise about a distinction first introduced in Day 2 but easy to lose in daily work: stewardship and ownership are not the same thing, and one without the other creates gaps. A steward who does not have a clearly named data owner above them has no one to escalate to when a conflict exceeds their authority. And an owner who has no steward below them has no one managing quality on the ground. Both roles need to be in place, and both need to know where the other sits.

Example: *A logistics organization appointed 23 "data stewards" as part of a governance initiative. Six months later, nothing had* *changed. The stewards had no time allocated to them, no decision-making rights, and no visible support from leadership. One steward said, "I have the title but not the authority. When I raise issues, people ignore me because they know there are no consequences." The organization reset by identifying the three people in each department who already fixed data problems informally - the ones people actually went to. They gave these individuals two hours per week of protected time, direct escalation paths to department heads, and visibility in weekly leadership reviews. Within a quarter, data issues were being caught and resolved 40% faster, not because of new people, but because existing problem-solvers finally had legitimate authority.*

Where stewardship is missing or symbolic, issues linger. Problems are noticed but not owned. The same discussions return. The same corrections follow. The same frustration builds. When stewardship is embedded, governance becomes self-correcting. Issues surface earlier. Conversations become easier. Trust grows steadily rather than in bursts.

This is subtle, but it is often the point where governance starts to hold.

Day 17

Audit and Validation

Stewardship creates ongoing responsibility. But even strong stewards need systematic ways to verify that data governance is holding. Responsibility without verification easily turns into assumption.

> *Trust is rarely lost because of a single failure.*
> *It erodes through uncertainty.*

Many organizations operate on informal confidence: if no one complains, the data must be fine. This works until it no longer does. When questions arise late, under pressure, or in front of senior leadership, confidence collapses quickly.

Audit and validation are often misunderstood as control mechanisms. In reality, they exist to replace guesswork with evidence. Not to catch people out, but to create a shared understanding of where governance is working and where it is not.

This day exists to address a common hesitation: the fear that validation will slow things down or create resistance. In reality, the opposite is often true. What slows organizations down is uncertainty or the absence of clarity. Validation, done well, reduces it.

From the 30 Days of Data Governance Posts

Data stewardship and quality checks are only part of the story. To really trust your data, you need regular audits and validation. These are the moments where you step back and ask, “Is our data really as accurate, complete, and consistent as we think?”

A strong audit and validation approach means you:

- Verify that data follows the definitions and standards you have set.
- Identify patterns of errors or recurring issues.
- Test processes to ensure they reliably produce correct data.
- Provide transparency and confidence to leaders and teams across the organization.
- Turn audits into a systematic, repeatable practice so your organization doesn’t rely on ad hoc checks.

When audit and validation become systematic, they help improve processes continuously, prevent recurring mistakes, and make trusted data an everyday reality, not a once-in-a-while reassurance.

Validation isn't just a checkpoint: it is a feedback loop.

Looking Back From Practice

Effective validation is predictable, not punitive. And it only creates value when it is systematic.

Ad hoc or reactive audits, triggered by a crisis, a complaint, or a leadership request, are better than nothing. But they do not change behavior. What changes behavior is regularity: a validation rhythm that teams expect, can prepare for, and participate in.

I have sat in more audit review meetings than I can count. Some were genuinely useful: issues surfaced, root causes discussed, actions assigned. Others were the same room, year after year: new dates at the top, same items underneath. Nobody was hiding anything. The issues had simply never been assigned to anyone with the authority and time to fix them.

In one organization, I remember asking the team lead responsible for (among other things) governance what had happened to the action points from the previous cycle. There was a pause. A little awkward silence. Then: "We logged them. But they were never picked up." The audit had done everything right, except for the one thing that mattered: it had produced findings without creating accountability.

This is the uncomfortable but important truth:
an audit without consequence is just documentation.

If issues are identified and nothing follows, no escalation, no accountability, no timeline for resolution, the message received is clear: the audit did not really matter.

People notice this quickly. The next time the audit comes around, they participate because the process exists, not because they expect anything to change. Cynicism sets in quickly. Teams learn that raising issues creates work without reward, and they stop raising them. The audit becomes a ritual rather than a tool.

Example: *A manufacturing company conducted quarterly "data audits" that everyone dreaded. Auditors would randomly sample records, find errors, and issue reports highlighting non-compliance. Teams viewed audits as "gotcha" exercises. Error rates never improved because people focused on hiding problems rather than fixing them. They replaced this with "data health checks", monthly 30-minute sessions where teams reviewed their own metrics using a standard checklist. Instead of external auditors finding problems, teams self-reported issues and proposed solutions. Leadership's role changed from judge to supporter: "What do you need to fix this?"*

Error rates dropped by 55% in six months, not because audits were stricter, but because they stopped being adversarial. Teams caught issues early when they were small, rather than hiding them until audits exposed them publicly.

The redesign in this example worked not only because the format changed, but because the consequence changed. When a team self-reported an issue, leadership responded by helping fix it, not by punishing. That response made honesty safe. And honesty, in a governance context, is what makes improvement possible.

When validation is routine and transparent, the tone changes. Patterns emerge. Root causes become visible. Conversations shift from blame to improvement. Validation becomes a way to improve continuously rather than a checkpoint, and governance becomes easier to sustain.

An audit that works quietly in the background is governance doing its job. The confidence it builds is invisible, but it is what turns the next decision from hesitation into action.

Day 18

Reporting and Dashboards

Validation confirms data quality behind the scenes. Reporting makes that quality visible or exposes its absence.

Most people in an organization do not engage with data governance directly. They never read policies. They rarely consult or engage with glossaries. They do not attend governance forums. What they do see every day are reports and dashboards.

This is where data governance becomes tangible, where trust is either reinforced or quietly undermined. A dashboard that is questioned forces people into defensive behavior: double-checking numbers, exporting data, recreating analyses. A trusted dashboard enables focus: discussion shifts from whether the data is right to what should be done about it.

This day exists because reporting is not the end of the data journey, but rather the point at which all upstream decisions are exposed. Definitions, ownership, quality, lineage, and processes all surface here, whether intentionally designed or not. This underlines a very simple truth:

Dashboards are not neutral artifacts. They are the most visible expression of data governance maturity.

From the 30 Days of Data Governance Posts

Data governance only matters if it shows up where decisions are made. That is why **reporting and dashboards** are such critical touchpoints: they are the front door to data for most people in the business. But flashy charts aren't enough. Governance needs to be embedded here too:

- Consistent definitions and metrics, so KPIs mean the same thing everywhere.
- Clear lineage and source transparency, ensuring users know where numbers come from.
- Built-in data quality indicators (green/amber/red) that show confidence levels at a glance.
- Dashboards that are designed not just to inform, but to drive the right actions.

When governance is embedded, leaders can trust what they see, act faster, and avoid endless debates about "which number is right." A report or dashboard is not just a pretty visualization. It is a decision-making tool.

Looking Back From Practice

When dashboards fail,
they fail socially before they fail technically.

People stop using them openly. They bring their own numbers into meetings. They preface insights with disclaimers. Over time, dashboards lose authority, even if the data is technically correct. The failure is not in the chart; it is in the trust that was never built around it.

There is a specific kind of dashboard failure I have seen more times than I can count, one that lands somewhere between funny and alarming before anyone in the room has quite decided which. It is the moment when a beautifully formatted executive dashboard shows that the largest sales in the quarter came from a product called "null." Or that the highest-revenue region is listed as "(blank)". Or that the top customer segment is coded as "-1". These are not edge cases. They are symptoms of data quality problems that were invisible until the moment the dashboard made them impossible to ignore. I have been in leadership meetings where someone pointed at "null" on a sales chart and said, in complete seriousness: "Who is this customer and why are they buying so much?" That moment, somewhere between amusing and deeply revealing, is often what finally triggers a real conversation about data governance.

A dashboard does not just display data.
It exposes everything upstream of it.

Example: *A technology company's executive dashboard showed the customer churn rate, but every leadership meeting began with 15 minutes of debate over the number. Marketing, Sales, and Customer Success all had different churn figures. The dashboard showed 8.3% monthly churn, but no one trusted it. The problem was not the calculation. It was that the dashboard did not show how churn was defined or which customers were included. They redesigned the dashboard to include: (1) a hover-over definition of "churned customer," (2) a data quality indicator showing what percentage of customers had complete data, and (3) a "methodology" link explaining inclusions and exclusions. They also added a comparison showing all three departmental methods side by side with explanations. Debates disappeared overnight. The dashboard went from "disputed" to "authoritative" without changing a single number, just by making the governance visible.*

Strong governance reverses this dynamic by embedding clarity directly into reporting. Ownership is visible. Quality is signaled. Lineage is understood. When this happens, when dashboards become decision instruments rather than debate triggers, something subtle shifts. Attention moves away from defending inputs and back towards discussing implications. The absence of debate about data correctness is not apathy - it is confidence. And that confidence is one of the strongest indicators that governance is working.

Day 19

Communication and Collaboration

Dashboards make data visible. Communication makes it understandable. Without both, governance remains theoretical.

Governance lives and dies in conversation.

No matter how carefully frameworks are designed, they cannot change behavior in isolation. People need to understand not only what is expected, but why and how it connects to their daily work.

Many data governance initiatives struggle because communication is treated as a final step rather than a core mechanism. Decisions are taken. Announcements are made. Documents are shared. And assumptions follow that understanding will spread automatically.

This day exists to challenge that assumption. To reframe communication and collaboration as foundational data governance practices, not supporting activities.

Governance does not embed through documentation. It embeds through dialogue, through explanation, feedback, and shared sense-making across functions.

From the 30 Days of Data Governance Posts

Even the most well-designed governance framework will fail if it lives in silence.

> *Communication and collaboration are the lifeblood of data governance.*

Without them, policies remain theory and ownership never sticks.

To make governance real, people need to talk about it, question it, and work on it together. That is where the culture shift begins: when governance is no longer "someone else's job" but part of everyday conversations.

Strong communication and collaboration show up in many ways:

- Common language: Shared definitions prevent endless debates and create clarity.

- Open feedback loops: Making it easy to raise data issues early before they grow costly.
- Cross-functional alignment: Business, IT, and compliance pulling in the same direction.
- Storytelling: Connecting governance to outcomes like smoother deliveries, faster reports, or happier customers builds energy and buy-in.

Communication builds understanding.

Collaboration builds ownership.

Together, they create the culture that makes governance sustainable, not a one-off initiative, but a way of working.

Looking Back From Practice

When things are genuinely working, silence is a sign of trust: people are not questioning the data because they do not need to. The silence that signals failure is different in texture; it is the silence of people who have stopped engaging because they have quietly concluded that the effort is not worth it. Learning to distinguish the two is one of the most important skills in governance leadership.

The most common governance failure is silence.

But not all silence is the same.

I have learned to pay attention to these signals early, not from the organizations that were visibly struggling, but from the ones that seemed fine. Governance forums were running. Reports were circulated. Attendance was reasonable. On the surface, everything was functioning.

But nobody was asking questions.

I remember a governance forum where I sat for ninety minutes without a single challenge, clarification, or concern raised from the floor. Policies were presented. Metrics were reviewed. Everyone nodded and left. Afterward, I asked one of the attendees what they thought of the session. "Useful" was their first response. Then, after a pause, "I mean, I'm not sure how it connects to what we actually do. But it was useful."

When people stop asking questions about governance decisions, it rarely means everything is clear. More often, it means they have decided the system is easier to bypass than to engage with. The silence is not the absence of opinions. It is the sound of disengagement. Governance has simply stopped being part of the conversation.

When people do not understand decisions, they work around them. When they are excluded from discussions, they withdraw. Governance stops feeling like shared work and starts *feeling like compliance*: a set of rules arriving from somewhere else, for reasons no one has explained.

Example: *A manufacturing company rolled out a new data governance framework with 73 pages of policies, three new committees, and five mandatory training sessions. Adoption was dreadful. Nine months later, the CDO asked why. One plant manager said, "We got told what to do, but not why it matters. Our bonus depends on production efficiency. How does data governance help with that?" The CDO reset the approach. Instead of pushing policies, they visited each plant and facilitated a 90-minute workshop asking: "What data problems cost you time or money?" Plant managers identified issues such as inaccurate inventory counts, which caused production delays, and quality data errors, triggering false product recalls. The CDO showed how governance addressed these specific problems. Suddenly, governance was no longer abstract compliance. It was a solution to their pain points. Adoption went from 23% to 87% in three months, not because policies changed, but because communication created relevance.*

What struck me most was not the size of the policy document or the number of committees created, but the reaction when communication finally changed. Once leaders began explaining decisions in practical terms - why rules existed, what problems they were solving, and how teams could raise concerns - participation shifted almost immediately. People who had previously ignored governance forums started showing up with questions and suggestions.

The lesson was simple: governance rarely fails because people disagree with it. It fails because people stop talking about it.

When conversation returns, governance often starts working again faster than expected. Alignment rarely needs to be rebuilt from scratch. It only needs to be reactivated.

Day 20

Training and Awareness

Communication creates understanding. Training turns understanding into capability.

But there is a gap between the two that most organizations underestimate.

Data Governance training tends to fail in a specific way. Not because the content is wrong, not because the slides are unclear, and not because people lack the motivation to learn. It fails because it teaches governance as a *concept* instead of showing it as a *situation*.

People handle data under time pressure, with competing priorities, and often without full context. In those moments, what matters is not what someone learned in a course three months earlier. It is whether they can recognize the situation in front of them and know what to do.

Under pressure, people fall back on what feels familiar: copying yesterday's spreadsheet, bypassing a validation step, or using the definition they have always used. Habits do not form through instruction alone, but through repetition in context. Training that does not put people in context does not build habits; it builds familiarity with language they cannot apply.

This day exists because data governance decays without continuous, relevant learning, especially as people change roles, systems are replaced, and priorities shift. Training and awareness are not a delivery milestone. They are how data governance stays alive in the people who carry it.

From the 30 Days of Data Governance Posts

Great governance doesn't happen by accident. People need to know what good data management looks like and how to do it. Training and awareness turn policies into practice, giving teams the knowledge and confidence to handle data responsibly every day.

Embedding governance into daily work requires more than just a manual. It requires skills, habits, and ongoing learning. Training programs and awareness initiatives help make governance tangible and actionable:

- Role-specific guidance: Tailored training for stewards, analysts, and leaders so everyone knows what's expected.

- Practical exercises: Hands-on examples that connect rules, definitions, and policies to real workflows.
- Regular refreshers: Short sessions, newsletters, or tips that reinforce knowledge and keep governance top-of-mind.
- Success stories: Highlighting wins shows the impact of good practices and motivates continuous improvement.

Training and awareness support governance, but they cannot carry it on their own.

Awareness is not a one-time event. It's an ongoing culture-building effort. When your teams understand the "why" and "how" of governance, compliance becomes natural, errors reduce, and trusted data becomes part of daily decisions.

Looking Back From Practice

I once sat in on a mandatory data governance training with a group of data stewards. The slides were clear. The policies were explained. The ownership model, the escalation paths, the stewardship responsibilities, all covered. Everyone completed the course. During the break, one steward turned to me and asked a simple question:

"If I receive a spreadsheet from another team and the numbers look wrong, what am I actually supposed to do?"

She was not resistant. She was confused. She had just sat through three hours of training and still could not answer the only question that would matter on Monday morning.

That question stayed with me. I started hearing versions of it in every training room I sat in afterward. Different words, same gap. The training had explained the structure of governance in accurate and reasonable detail. It had never shown what governance looked like at the moment when a person faced a decision under pressure.

Training works when people recognize themselves in it, not in the roles, but in the situations.

The quiet question in every disengaged training room is the same: *"What does this actually mean for my work tomorrow morning?"* When no one can answer that question, attention drifts. Not because people disagree. Because they cannot see the connection.

Generic sessions create familiarity, not capability.

Familiarity is knowing what data stewardship means. Capability is knowing what to do when the spreadsheet arrives and the numbers look wrong.

Example: *A financial services firm required all employees to complete a 4-hour "Data Governance Fundamentals" e-learning course. Completion rates were high, 98%. Behavior did not change. Post-training surveys showed people could recite policies and* *principles but did not know how to apply them. They redesigned the training to be role-specific and scenario-based: analysts received 45-minute workshops on "How to validate data sources for executive reports"; operations staff received 30-minute sessions on "Handling customer data correctly in daily transactions"; managers received case studies on "Making decisions when data quality is uncertain"; data owners received focused sessions on "How to support my stewards and make decisions within my domain." The content was shorter, but it was anchored in what each group actually did. Six months later, data incident reports dropped by 62%. When asked, employees could explain not just what the policies were, but why they mattered for their specific work. The difference was not the content. It was the point of view.*

What changed was not what data governance required of people, but the angle from which it was explained. Instead of teaching data governance as a concept, the training showed how it appeared inside everyday work, inside the decisions, the pressures, and the shortcuts that people faced.

People rarely change their behavior because a rule was explained more clearly. They change when they recognize the moment in which the rule applies, when they see their own situation reflected in the scenario clearly enough to think: *that is exactly what happens to me.*

That is when training stops producing familiarity and starts building judgment. It is also when data governance stops depending on enforcement and begins sustaining itself.

Part 4 Recap

Your Turn

This part was about making governance operational rather than theoretical. Stewardship, validation, reporting, communication, training - the mechanisms through which intent becomes habit. The questions below are most useful when answered honestly: not as an audit of what is in place, but as a read of what is actually working.

1. Who is already acting as a steward without the title?

They exist in most organizations. The person others turn to when something does not look right. The one who quietly keeps the unofficial source of truth. The one who already knows which data can be trusted and which cannot. Governance that formalizes these existing behaviors tends to work better than governance that creates new responsibilities from scratch.

2. Are audits in your organization something people dread or something people use?

The answer to this question says a great deal about whether governance is experienced as oversight or support. If the honest answer is dread, the mechanism probably needs to change before the frequency does.

3. What do people argue about in meetings that they should not have to argue about?

If meetings regularly include debate about whether a number is right, whose version to use, or what a metric actually means, that is governance work waiting to be done. Not because the debate is wrong, but because it should have been resolved before the meeting started.

4. Where is data governance still something people have to remember to do, instead of something built into how the work happens?

That is often the clearest sign that governance has not yet become operational. What people must remember under pressure is easy to skip. What is built into the work is far more likely to hold.

When data governance is embedded in daily work, it stops requiring an act of faith. People do not have to trust it consciously anymore. They just use it. That is what the beginning of organizational confidence looks like.

Governance settles in when it reduces friction rather than adds it. If any of these questions reveal that data governance currently creates more work than it resolves, that is the most useful thing you can know at this stage.

Part 5

Advanced Practices and Strategic Impact

Once governance is embedded, a new question naturally emerges:

How far can this take us?

This part exists to explore what becomes possible when the basics are in place and working. Advanced practices such as master data management, metadata, lineage, privacy, and enabling technology are not starting points. They are multipliers. That distinction matters: a multiplier applied to a weak foundation produces a bigger problem faster. Applied to a strong one, it produces scale, resilience, and adaptability at a speed that was not possible before.

Too often, organizations jump here too early and wonder why complexity increases instead of value. Tools are implemented before agreements are made. Automation accelerates inconsistency instead of reducing it.

This part reframes advanced practices as strategic leverage. When built on clear ownership, shared definitions, and trusted processes, they allow organizations to operate with greater confidence as complexity deepens and stakes rise.

The focus here is not sophistication for its own sake, but sustainability and scalability: governance that can grow with the organization instead of breaking under it.

The practices in this part are not starting points. They become possible once trust has been established and confidence has begun to form, marking the point where governance stops explaining itself and starts delivering. They are not simply more complex versions of what came before. They emerge when the foundations hold.

Day 21

Master Data Management

Once governance is embedded, organizations can build on that foundation with practices that extend and strengthen confidence across teams and systems.

Advanced practices often attract organizations early in their governance journey. The promise is appealing: consistency, scale, and control. Master Data Management (MDM) is often seen as the answer to inconsistency. What it tends to do first is reveal governance weaknesses. Without agreement on ownership, definitions, and decision rights, technology makes disagreement more visible than resolving it.

Organizations often introduce Master Data Management at exactly the wrong moment: when inconsistency has already taken hold, showing up in multiple customer views, conflicting product hierarchies, or duplicated suppliers. The symptoms are real, and the pressure to "fix it properly" is high. MDM sells the idea of order, control, and a single source of truth, a reassuring idea when complexity feels unmanageable. What organizations often underestimate is that MDM is not primarily a data problem. It is a decision problem.

The challenge starts well before technology enters the picture. The more fundamental questions come first and need answers: "Who decides what a customer is?" "Who resolves conflicts when different parts of the organization disagree?" "Which use cases take precedence when definitions collide?" Without shared answers, MDM does not resolve fragmentation; it formalizes it.

This day exists to reposition MDM as a governance accelerator, not a shortcut. It is meant to challenge the reflex to reach for MDM before the harder governance questions have been resolved.

MDM amplifies whatever governance maturity already exists.

The underlying pattern is simple: where ownership is clear, it creates scale. Where ownership is weak, it creates conflict with better tooling.

From the 30 Days of Data Governance Posts

After embedding governance into daily work, it is time to take a step further: turning good practices into organizational leverage.

MDM is about creating a single, consistent view of your key entities, the critical data that underpins your business, like customers, products, suppliers, or locations. Without it, reports, dashboards, and decisions risk being built on conflicting or incomplete information.

Strong MDM practices mean you:

- Define and govern key entities across systems so everyone "speaks the same data language".
- Centralize or synchronize critical records to eliminate duplicates and discrepancies.
- Ensure data quality at the source to prevent errors from propagating downstream.
- Enable reliable reporting and analytics to power confident, strategic decisions.
- Ensure data quality at the source. Yes, already mentioned above, but still worth repeating: high-quality master data starts at the point of entry, preventing errors from propagating across systems and ensuring trusted decisions.

Master data is the authoritative reference for your organization's critical entities. It is the foundation on which all operational and analytical systems rely to remain consistent and accurate.

Looking Back From Practice

Successful MDM initiatives start with difficult conversations, not system design. In practice, that work has to come first.

When organizations align on what constitutes a customer, a product, or a supplier, and on who decides when conflicts arise, technology becomes an enabler. When they do not, MDM becomes a source of frustration. Governance determines which path is taken.

Those pre-MDM conversations have a particular quality that I have come to recognize. They tend to start confidently. Everyone in the room believes the answer is obvious. Then they stall the moment someone asks a question that sounds simple but is not: "When a company has five subsidiaries and they all buy from us, how many customers is that?" The silence that follows is not ignorance. It is the realization that different parts of the business have been operating on different answers for years, each one locally rational, and that no one has ever been required to choose. That is the moment MDM really begins. Not when the vendor is selected, but when the organization accepts that it has to make a decision it has been deferring.

Example: *A global retailer spent €4.2 million implementing an MDM system for "customer." Eighteen months after launch, they had three MDM systems running in parallel because different business units could not agree on the definition. E-commerce wanted "customer" to mean anyone with an online account. Retail* *stores wanted it to mean anyone with a loyalty card. B2B wanted it to mean corporate purchasing entities. The MDM system could absolutely handle all three, but leadership had never decided which definition was authoritative for which purpose. Result: three separate systems, continued conflicts, and €4.2M with no ROI. They finally convened a six-month "Customer Definition Council" with representatives from all divisions plus the CFO as tiebreaker. Once they agreed that "household" was the master entity (with sub-entities for individuals, accounts, and corporate relationships), the technical implementation took eight weeks. The governance work took six months, but that is what actually worked.*

In my experience, the hardest work happens before any technical architecture is agreed upon. It takes shape when business leaders realize that they can no longer optimize for their own version of "truth" without creating friction elsewhere. Trade-offs have to be made explicit, and someone has to be given the authority to decide.

Too often, this step is skipped and organizations pay for it later. MDM becomes a battleground. Data models grow more complex, exceptions multiply, and trust erodes, not because the technology is poor, but because the governance beneath it is unresolved.

When MDM works well, it rarely feels dramatic. What changes first is stability. Less time reconciling. Fewer late-stage escalations. No more debates about which number is correct. And over time, that stability is what allows an organization to scale without drowning in its own data.

Day 22

Metadata and Lineage

Master data provides consistency for entities. Metadata and lineage provide transparency for understanding.

As data ecosystems grow, understanding quietly erodes. More sources, more transformations, more consumers, and fewer people who can confidently explain how a number was produced. This is where trust starts to crack.

New systems are added. Transformations multiply. Data products are reused in ways their creators never anticipated. Over time, almost no one can explain where a number comes from, only that it "usually looks right".

Metadata and lineage are too often positioned as documentation. In reality, they are about restoring transparency and confidence under scrutiny, especially when decisions are challenged, numbers are questioned, or accountability suddenly matters. In those moments, trust hinges on the ability to explain, calmly and credibly, how data came to be.

This day exists to position traceability as a prerequisite for confidence, not an optional enhancement. Without metadata and lineage, organizations rely on personal memory and institutional folklore. With them, explanation becomes part of the system rather than a heroic effort.

From the 30 Days of Data Governance Posts

Ever wondered why understanding your data is not just about the data itself, but also its journey? This is another piece of the whole data puzzle. Metadata and lineage make your data **transparent, traceable, and trustworthy**, giving teams the **confidence to act**.

Key aspects to focus on:

- Data lineage: Trace the path from source to report, uncovering transformations and dependencies.
- Metadata clarity: Understand attributes, definitions, and ownership for every dataset.
- Control and audit: Identify where issues originate and how they propagate.
- Enhance collaboration: Shared metadata and lineage reduce debate and rework across teams.
- Ensure data quality at the source: Yes, it's worth saying again: accurate source data makes metadata meaningful and lineage reliable, so your insights are trustworthy.

Key takeaways:

- **Metadata describes your data:** what it represents, who owns it, and how it should be used.
- **Lineage traces the journey of data:** through systems and processes.
- **Metadata and lineage go hand in hand**: one without the other limits clarity and trust.

While my personal preference is for master data, metadata and lineage are essential parts of the bigger picture.

Looking Back From Practice

Transparency matters most the moment a number is questioned.

When everything is running smoothly, no one asks where a number came from. The question surfaces when something looks wrong, when a decision is challenged, or when leadership needs to explain a result to a board or a regulator. Under that pressure, often public, the ability to trace data from source to conclusion determines whether confidence can be restored quickly or whether weeks of investigation follow. I have been in both kinds of meetings. The difference in tone is striking.

Lineage is rarely discussed when things go well. It becomes critical when decisions are challenged. At that moment, transparency determines how quickly confidence can be restored.

When lineage is embedded, explanation becomes routine rather than reactive. Questions can be answered clearly: where the data came from, how it was transformed, and why a number looks the way it does.

Lineage is not about satisfying curiosity.
It is about protecting decision-makers.

Example: *A pharmaceutical company's board questioned why R&D spending had apparently increased by 18% quarter over quarter. The CFO could not explain it. Finance analysts spent over ten days tracing it back through seven transformation steps across four systems. They discovered that a change in currency conversion logic two months earlier had inadvertently double-counted costs for European trials. The error cost them €3.2M in misallocated budget. Worse, the delay in identifying the cause led the board to lose confidence in all financial reporting for six months. They implemented automated lineage tracking that documented every transformation with before/after snapshots. Four months later, when board members questioned a revenue figure, the CFO pulled up the lineage in real-time during the meeting, showed exactly how the number was calculated, and identified that the question stemmed from a timing difference (not an error). The meeting moved on in two minutes instead of generating weeks of* *investigation. Lineage did not prevent questions; it answered them instantly.*

Lineage changes the tone of conversations in daily conversations. When questions arise, teams move from defensive explanations to shared investigation. Accountability shifts from individuals to processes.

Where lineage is absent, organizations compensate with caution. Decisions slow down. Escalations increase. Trust becomes personal rather than institutional, held together by individuals who happen to remember, rather than systems that are designed to know.

When lineage is embedded, confidence scales. Not because every path is perfect, but because explanations are available when they matter most. Progressively, that transparency becomes a quiet stabilizer, something organizations only fully appreciate once it is missing.

There is one dimension of lineage that I find myself discussing more frequently now, and which did not feature in the original series: "What happens when the data feeds a model rather than a report?"

When an AI system makes a recommendation, a credit decision, a hiring shortlist, a clinical flag, the question, "Where did this come from?" does not go away. It becomes more consequential. A human decision maker can explain their reasoning. A model cannot do that on its own. Lineage is what makes explanation possible, tracing not just the data that trained it, but the transformations, filters, and assumptions that shaped what the model learned.

I have been in rooms where a leadership team approved the deployment of a machine learning model without being able to answer two basic governance questions: whose data was it, and what happened to it between source and model input? At that point, the organization has not reduced uncertainty; it has accelerated it. Quietly, and with great technical confidence.

This is not a warning against AI. It is the same principle that runs through this entire book: technology amplifies whatever governance maturity already exists. A model built on lineage that is understood, owned, and traceable is a model whose outputs can be explained, challenged, and trusted. A model built on data no one can account for is a governance problem with a very sophisticated front end.

Lineage, in the age of AI, is still not documentation. It is an accountability infrastructure.

These questions return in Day 30, where AI raises the stakes further.

Day 23

Data Privacy and Compliance

Transparency about data is essential. But transparency must be balanced with protection.

Privacy and compliance are often experienced as external pressure rather than internal responsibility. Regulation arrives from the outside. Deadlines are imposed. Audits demand evidence. Governance is framed as protection against penalties instead of the enablement of trust.

In that framing, compliance becomes something to endure rather than integrate.

This day exists to challenge that mindset. To reframe compliance as part of trustworthy data practice enables confident use instead of restricting it.

In mature organizations, privacy is not treated as an exception layer added at the end. It is embedded into how data is defined, accessed, and used. That integration reduces both risk and hesitation, because people know where boundaries are before they are tested.

When privacy is unclear, organizations default to extremes: either excessive restrictions that block value or informal workarounds that increase risk. Governance is what allows a more balanced, sustainable position.

From the 30 Days of Data Governance Posts

Data governance protects your organization's data not just for efficiency, but also for trust and legal compliance. Privacy and compliance are not obstacles: they are safeguards that allow your data to be used confidently.

A few important points to consider:

- Policies and rules: Define what is allowed, how data should be handled, and who is responsible.
- Training and awareness: A kind reminder from Day 20: ensure your teams understand privacy obligations and compliance requirements.
- Risk mitigation: Identify sensitive data, monitor usage, and have processes for issues or breaches.
- Control and audit: Track compliance over time to ensure rules are followed and risks minimized.

A few things to keep in mind:

- Privacy and compliance are enablers, not blockers. They build trust and protect your organization.
- Policies are only effective if people know them and put them into practice.
- Monitoring and auditing make governance sustainable.

Looking Back From Practice

Privacy and compliance usually break down not because organizations do not care about them, but because the right behavior is harder to carry out consistently than the wrong one. Policies exist, but processes do not support them. Responsibilities are defined, but escalation paths remain unclear. People want to do the right thing, but lack guidance under pressure.

The moment I pay most attention to in privacy and compliance work is not the violation itself. It is the moment just before it, when someone knows the compliant route but does not take it, not out of carelessness, but because the compliance path feels too slow, too unclear, or too impractical for the reality of the work.

The patterns appear differently depending on context, but the structure remains the same. In manufacturing, the compliant path may lose to operational speed: a worker under production pressure skips a required data entry step because the line cannot wait. In financial services, the gap is more likely between what compliance requires and what client-facing staff can explain: the rule is followed until a client pushes back, and then it starts to dissolve. In logistics and services, failures tend to occur at hand-off points, where data moves between teams or systems, and no one is clearly accountable for what happens in transit. Different surfaces. The same underlying problem: the right behavior has not been made easier than the wrong one. Governance is treated as a layer added on top of work, rather than built into how work happens.

The most frustrating version: when an organization has genuinely invested in compliance, training, policies, signage, and reminders, and violations continue because the compliant path is simply harder than the non-compliant one. That is not a culture problem. It is a process design problem. And it cannot be solved by more training.

Example: *A healthcare organization faced GDPR fines after employees emailed patient records to external partners without encryption. The organization had clear policies prohibiting this, mandatory annual training, and visible reminders. Yet violations continued. When they investigated, they found that the approved secure file-sharing system was so cumbersome (requiring 11 clicks and two-factor authentication each time) that staff used email because it was faster, even though patients were waiting. The organization did not increase training or tighten policies; they fixed the process. A one-click secure sharing button was implemented directly in the patient record system with automatic encryption and* *audit logging. Violations dropped from 40 per month to 2 per month within 12 weeks and remained at that level through a period of close monitoring. Compliance improved not because people cared more, but because* ***doing the right thing became easier than doing the wrong thing.***

When privacy governance is built into processes and roles, it stops feeling like an additional burden. Behavior changes subtly. Questions are raised earlier. Assumptions are challenged. Boundaries are clearer. Decisions are made with greater confidence because people understand what is allowed, what is not, and why.

The real benefit is not just reduced risk. It also lowers hesitation and friction simultaneously. When the compliance path is also the easier path, people stop deliberating about what they are allowed to do and simply do the right thing. That is when compliance stops being a burden and starts being part of how work gets done.

Day 24

Data Governance Technology

Privacy protects data. When used well, technology scales governance. When used poorly, it scales confusion instead.

Technology often enters the governance conversation early because it feels concrete. Tools, such as data catalogs, lineage tools, quality platforms, and master data systems, promise structure, visibility, control, and automation. Faced with growing complexity, many organizations see these tools as the natural starting point.

> *Data governance technology rarely solves governance problems on its own.*

Tools do not create ownership. They do not resolve disagreements about definitions. They do not decide which data should be trusted or who is responsible when it is not.

What technology does is **amplify whatever practices already exist**.

When roles are clear and processes are understood, tools make governance easier to scale. When those foundations are missing, technology simply makes the confusion more visible.

This day exists to address a common misunderstanding: treating the purchase of governance technology as a milestone. In reality, technology is not the beginning of governance maturity; it is the result of it.

Governance technology does not create clarity. It reflects it. When introduced too early, tools make confusion more visible and more permanent. When introduced at the right time, they amplify shared understanding and reduce manual effort.

The real question is not which tool to buy, but what behavior the tool is meant to support.

From the 30 Days of Data Governance Posts

Data governance is not just about rules and roles. Ok, I'll say it: the right technology can make the difference between theory and practice. BUT tools should *support* your strategy, *not dictate* it. The focus is on enabling teams to manage, access, and trust their data efficiently.

Watch these key areas:

- Data management platforms, looking at centralizing data assets, master data, and metadata.
- Automated quality checks flag inconsistencies and reduce manual errors – but only where the underlying process is already stable (see Day 12 on automation sequencing).
- Collaborative features, where workflows, approvals, and annotations that embed governance into daily work can be of great support.
- Reporting and analytics, where dashboards and alerts make trusted data actionable (and yes, analytics is not just about reporting and dashboards, but so much more...).

Technology alone won't resolve your problems unless you have a very clear view of what you are facing and have done the full homework.

Hint: read the earlier posts again before Day 24.

A tool is just a tool, and a fool with a tool is still a fool.

Remember: tools are enablers, not a replacement for processes, communication, and training.

Looking Back From Practice

Technology can be a powerful accelerator. It can also become an expensive distraction. Tools can make governance more operational, but not necessarily more effective.

I have watched this happen more than once: organizations celebrate the launch of a new governance platform as if governance itself had been implemented. Dashboards were configured, catalogs populated, and lineage diagrams produced. Yet the most important questions remained unanswered: who owns the data, which definitions matter, and who decides when something is wrong. Predictably, usage dropped off.

Without those answers, the tool had very little to amplify.

Technology does not create governance.

It exposes whether governance is already in place.

When tools are introduced before agreement, adoption suffers. When they reinforce shared practices, they accelerate maturity. Sequence matters more than features. In governance, technology rarely creates discipline. More often, it reinforces whatever discipline already exists.

Example: *A media company spent €1.5M on a comprehensive data catalog tool that could automatically discover data assets, map lineage, and track quality scores. After 18 months, usage was at*

11%. At best. The tool worked perfectly, but no one used it. Why? Because the organization had not agreed on basic definitions or ownership. The catalog showed that "customer_id" appeared in forty-seven datasets, but could not tell users which was authoritative because that decision had never been made. Analysts continued using spreadsheets because those had the context that the tool lacked. The organization paused the technology initiative for six months and focused on governance fundamentals: defining 20 critical data elements, assigning clear owners, and documenting authoritative sources. Once those agreements existed, they turned the tool back on. Usage jumped to 76% within three months because now the tool reflected decisions people trusted, rather than highlighting confusion they could not resolve.

The most successful governance tools are boring. They are used quietly, consistently, and without fanfare. They reinforce agreements that already exist and make good behavior easier. Where tools fail, it is seldom because of functionality. It is misalignment. Processes are unclear. Ownership is disputed. Expectations are implicit.

Technology strengthens maturity - or immaturity.

That is why sequencing matters more than features. And why governance decisions should always precede tooling decisions.

One category of tooling deserves a specific note, because it is arriving faster than most governance teams are prepared for: AI-assisted governance tools.

A growing number of data catalog and quality platforms now use machine learning to automatically discover data assets, suggest classifications, flag anomalies, and propose definitions. On the surface, this sounds like exactly what overworked governance teams need. In practice, it introduces a new version of the same sequencing problem this chapter is about.

An AI tool that auto-classifies your data assets will produce output as trustworthy as the governance context in which it operates. If ownership is unclear, the suggested owner will be unclear. If definitions are contested, the suggested definitions will reflect the loudest pattern in the data, not the agreed-upon truth. I have seen organizations treat AI-generated data catalogs as finished governance because the tool was confident, the dashboards were populated, and the work looked done. It was not done. It had simply moved faster toward the same unresolved questions.

The principle holds: tools amplify what already exists. AI tools do it faster, at a greater scale, and sometimes with more authority than the underlying agreement warrants.

Use them, but use them after the human agreements are in place, not as a substitute for making them.

Day 25

Continuous Improvement

What keeps governance relevant over time is not stability, but the ability to adapt without losing coherence.

Continuous improvement is not a phase at the end of implementation. It is what keeps data governance connected to reality through leadership changes, acquisitions, pressure, and the drift that happens when priorities shift and no one is watching.

Governance does not prevent change. Organizations change regardless. Systems evolve. People move. Business priorities shift. What worked last year can quietly become outdated. Without deliberate reflection, governance begins to drift; not because it was wrong at the start, but because the organization kept moving and the governance around it did not.

That is why continuous improvement matters. Not as optimization. Not as a maturity exercise. But as the practice of keeping governance connected to reality over time. Mature governance recognizes that clarity must be revisited, not assumed. Feedback must be collected, not inferred. What once worked still needs to be tested against what the organization has become.

Improvement is not a phase at the end of implementation; it is what keeps governance relevant. It is what allows governance to adapt without losing coherence, and what makes it possible for the organization to keep relying on it.

From the 30 Days of Data Governance Posts

Data Governance is not something you implement once. It is something you *continuously cultivate.*

Organizations evolve, technologies shift, people change roles, and your governance needs to grow along with it.

It is not about chasing perfection.
It is about building adaptability.

Strong governance is a mindset of **learning**, **refining**, and **evolving over time**, and most importantly, keeping it embedded in reality, solving real challenges that teams face every day.

Here's how to keep that momentum alive:

- Regular assessments: Measure adoption, data quality, and maturity. Track not just compliance, but impact.

- Feedback loops: Listen to your users, data owners, and stewards. They often see what governance frameworks miss. Be ready to adjust.
- Learn from exceptions: Every issue, escalation, or workaround tells you where to simplify, automate, or clarify.
- Celebrate small wins: Highlight progress, not just policies. Recognition fuels engagement.
- Adapt roles and responsibilities: Governance is not static; it matures as your organization does.

The best data governance programs are those that learn (I use the word program deliberately. "Program" implies structure, commitment, and iteration, not just a project with a start and an end date).

They evolve from project to practice, from compliance to culture. They turn governance from something you "must do" into something you "want to do", because it makes work smarter, faster, and more trusted. How do you ensure your governance keeps evolving rather than stagnating? What mechanisms do you have in place to keep it relevant and resilient as your organization grows?

Sometimes the real success isn't in the framework you built, but in how it keeps improving, adapting, and inspiring others to take part.

The next phase of this journey is all about that connection: how governance translates into long-term value and purpose.

It is NOT about frameworks on paper; it is about creating systems that solve real problems and keep delivering value over time.

Looking Back From Practice

When organizations treat governance as a delivered project rather than a living system, the pattern is familiar. The launch energy is real. Policies are defined. Roles are clear. And then, gradually, the momentum fades. Adoption plateaus. Workarounds begin to reappear. Within two or three years, the framework needs to be substantially rebuilt, not because it was wrong, but because it stayed still while the organization kept moving.

The effort is never entirely lost. But much of it has to be redone. That is an expensive way to learn.

What separates organizations that sustain governance from those that do not is rarely the quality of the initial design. I have seen beautifully designed governance models lose traction within a year, while simpler ones continued to work. The difference is the habit of reflection.

Organizations that sustain governance build in small, deliberate check-ins. Not formal reviews, but honest and practical questions asked by people doing the work: What has changed since we defined this? Where does this process no longer match reality? Which rule made sense twelve months ago but now creates friction? These moments are not escalations. They are adjustments. Without them, governance drifts away from how work actually happens. The documentation remains. The organization has moved on.

This is not a failure of governance design. It is a failure to treat governance as something that needs tending.

Example: *A logistics company had excellent governance for their domestic operations, with clear roles, trusted data, and smooth processes. Then they acquired a company in Asia. They tried to impose their existing governance framework: the same roles, the same standards, the same tools. It failed spectacularly. Local teams ignored the framework because it did not fit their regulatory environment, business model, or language. After nine months of frustration, the governance team spent three weeks in Asia just listening. They discovered that while the principles were sound (clear ownership, quality standards, defined processes), the implementation needed to flex. They kept the global principles but allowed regional adaptation: definitions could vary if clearly documented, tools could differ if they were properly integrated, and processes could adjust to local context if outcomes remained consistent. Compliance rose from 31% to 88% in six months, not because they enforced harder, but because they learned and adapted.*

In most cases, this often comes down to a small set of recurring questions. What has changed since we last defined this? Where are we still compensating manually? And which decisions are we making today with less confidence than before? The organizations that improve are the ones that ask these questions regularly, not as a formal exercise, but as part of how they work.

What emerges is resilience, not something designed in, but something that is built through practice. Governance stops being fragile. It adapts without losing coherence. That adaptability is what allows organizations to scale without having to repeatedly start over. Improvement sustains trust more effectively than control ever can.

What continuous improvement ultimately builds is not better data governance. It is durable confidence. The kind that holds under pressure, survives leadership changes, and compounds over time.

The work is not to perfect data governance, but to keep it close enough to reality that people continue to use it.

Your Turn

The practices in this part, master data management, metadata, lineage, privacy, technology, continuous improvement, are often where organizations arrive too early. The questions below are designed to reveal whether the foundations beneath them are solid enough to hold their weight.

1. What problem are you trying to solve with technology right now?

Not the tool you are evaluating, but the behavior you hope the tool will support. If the answer is unclear or involves resolving disagreements that governance has not yet resolved, the tool will likely accelerate confusion rather than reduce it.

2. Can you explain how your most important number was produced?

Pick one. Revenue. Churn. Customer count. Active users. Whoever is responsible for that number: can they trace it, step by step, from source to dashboard? If not, lineage work has not started yet. And when that number gets challenged in a board meeting, that absence will be visible.

3. Where has governance become outdated without anyone noticing?

Definitions drift. Roles change. Processes evolve. The governance documentation often does not keep up. This is not a failure; it is normal. But normal does not mean consequence-free. The question is which outdated element is currently causing the most silent confusion.

4. What would tell you that governance is improving, not just expanding?

There is a difference between governance growing larger and governance growing better. Maturity does not mean more policies, more roles, or more tools. It means the same quality with less effort, fewer escalations, and faster resolution. That distinction is worth holding onto as complexity increases.

What would it take for those advanced practices to actually work in your organization today? If the answer depends on foundations that are not yet in place, that is useful to know. These practices do not create maturity on their own; they reveal whether it is already there.

A note of caution: Before applying the practices in this part, ask whether the foundations are truly in place. The advanced practices in Part 5 amplify what exists beneath them. If ownership is unclear, definitions are contested, or quality is unpredictable, the tools and techniques here will likely deepen confusion, not reduce it. That is not a reason to wait indefinitely; it is a reason to be honest about where the foundations need strengthening first.

PART 6

Connecting Governance to Business Value

Governance ultimately lives or dies by one measure: does it help the business move forward?

This part exists to make that connection clear. To show how governance, when done well, accelerates decisions, reduces risk, aligns teams, and shapes culture, not as a side effect, but as its core purpose.

At this stage, governance stops being something the organization has and becomes something the organization uses. The value is no longer theoretical. It starts to show up in faster decisions, clearer alignment, earlier visibility of risk, and greater confidence in the actions that follow.

The chapters in this part connect governance directly to outcomes leaders care about: speed, cost, alignment, and culture. They show that these are not downstream benefits, but evidence that governance is doing its job.

This is where governance stops needing to justify itself and starts being used. Where the original question finds its answer, not in theory, but in the ability to act.

This final part brings the journey full circle: from trust in data to trust in decisions and from governance as structure to governance as value.

Day 26

Faster, Smarter Decisions

Continuous improvement keeps governance relevant. But relevance only matters if governance creates tangible value. The first and most visible value is decision speed.

> *Organizations often frame speed and control as opposites. Move fast, or be careful, but not both.*

In reality, what slows decisions is rarely governance. It is the absence of clarity. It is uncertainty. When data cannot be trusted, every decision carries hidden risk. Leaders compensate by asking for more validation, more reassurance, more time. What looks like thoroughness is often hesitation in disguise.

> *Speed emerges not from pressure, but from confidence.*

And confidence is the specific thing data governance creates and the reason it is worth the slower work.

When ownership is clear, definitions are shared, and data quality is predictable, decisions change character. They do not become reckless; they become calmer. Less energy is spent debating inputs, more on understanding implications.

This day exists to show how trust, not bureaucracy, accelerates action. It reframes decision speed as an outcome of trust, not urgency. Governance does not push organizations to move faster. It removes the reasons they slow themselves down.

From the 30 Days of Data Governance Posts

We've reached the final stretch of the journey: ***Connecting Governance to Business Value.***

Because in the end, governance is not about rules, policies, or frameworks. It is about helping the business move faster, with confidence and clarity.

Too often, governance gets a bad reputation for slowing things down. More approvals. More checkpoints. More "Wait until the data is fixed."

But done right, it is actually the opposite.

Governance is what clears the path.

When people share the same definitions, trust the same metrics, and know who owns what, decisions stop getting stuck in endless discussions. That is when governance turns *from control into acceleration*. From red tape to green light.

Here is how it shows up in practice:

- Trusted data: No more debating which source to use. Everyone can act on the same numbers.
- Clear roles: Data ownership is understood, so responsibility doesn't get lost in silos.
- Standardized processes: Data collection, validation, and reporting happen consistently, reducing rework.
- Visible metrics: Dashboards and KPIs give teams confidence to make fast, informed decisions.

Good governance does not create extra steps. It removes confusion, duplication, and risk.

It builds **trust in data**, so teams can act decisively.

Clarity enables speed. The better your governance, the faster your organization can turn insight into action.

Looking Back From Practice

When governance works, it disappears.

Decision-making feels almost unremarkable. That disappearance is easy to miss, precisely because nothing dramatic happens. There is no moment of visible success equivalent to the visible failure it replaced. That is often one of the clearest signs that governance is doing its job. At this point, the noise begins to fall away. Debates shift from inputs to implications. Fewer pre-meetings to align numbers. Less hedging in presentations. Less 'just to be safe' delay. Decisions are still discussed, challenged, and refined, but they move forward.

What changes is how meetings feel. People arrive having already seen the same numbers. Conversations begin where they should begin - on the interpretation, not the input. Someone can say “revenue was down 7% in the North” without the next three exchanges being about whether the 7% figure is trustworthy. They move on to what the number actually means. The difference is quiet, but for anyone who has sat through months of the alternative, it is unmistakable.

I have found that the people who feel the value of governance most acutely are often not the senior leaders who commissioned it, but the analysts and middle managers who used to spend their Fridays reconciling numbers before the Monday morning review. When that work stops being necessary, they notice immediately. And they will tell you, unprompted, that they have more time to think now - to look at what the numbers actually mean rather than whether they are right. Where analytical energy goes is one of the clearest signals that governance has taken hold.

Example: *A consumer goods company's monthly business reviews routinely ran four hours, with the first 80 minutes spent reconciling different versions of sales data. Finance, Sales, and Marketing each brought their own numbers. Once governance established a single authoritative sales reporting process with clear ownership (the Revenue Operations team) and visible data quality indicators, that 80-minute reconciliation disappeared. Reviews dropped to 2.5 hours, with time reallocated to strategic discussions about market response and competitive positioning. The CMO noted, "We used to spend most of the meeting arguing about the past. Now we spend it planning the future." The data had not become perfect; it had become predictable. That predictability was what gave them permission to move forward.*

What changes next is not only speed but the quality of the conversation. Action replaces verification. Speed emerges as a consequence of trust. What changes most is the tone. Conversations become less defensive. People argue about direction rather than data. Over time, the effect compounds. Teams gain momentum. Leaders trust what they see. The organization becomes more responsive without becoming chaotic.

This is what governance at its best often looks like in everyday work. Not louder. Not more visible. Just less friction where friction used to be.

Speed, in this sense, is not about moving quickly. It is about not being slowed down by doubt.

Day 27

Reducing Risk and Cost

Faster decisions create competitive advantage. But speed without safety creates exposure. Governance protects the bottom line by reducing both, and organizations that understand this early spend far less time reacting to problems they could have prevented.

Risk thrives in ambiguity. Inconsistent data, unclear processes, undefined ownership, and hidden dependencies increase exposure. And they are not just governance issues. They are risk multipliers. Problems remain hidden until they surface under pressure, often when correction is expensive or politically difficult. Governance reduces risk by making expectations explicit.

Across industries and organizations of every size, the same pattern appears: the cost of uncertainty is quietly underestimated. Rework, reconciliation, duplicated analysis, late escalations: individually manageable, collectively draining. These costs rarely appear in a single budget line. They are distributed across teams, absorbed into "how things work around here", and rarely traced back to their root cause: data people could not fully trust.

This day exists to make that cost visible. To connect trust directly to financial and operational resilience. Not as a fear-based argument, but as a recognition that governance reduces exposure by setting expectations clear before they are tested.

From the 30 Days of Data Governance Posts

Good data governance doesn't just make life easier; it **protects your bottom line**.

Every decision in an organization carries risk. Inaccurate or inconsistent data can lead to costly mistakes: wrong forecasts, regulatory breaches, and misallocated resources. You name it. *Governance is your safety net.*

It is not about adding bureaucracy. It is about **creating confidence**. When data is trustworthy, processes are clear, and ownership is defined, teams can act decisively, without second-guessing or duplication of effort.

Here's how it works in practice:

- Error prevention: Clear rules, validation steps, and agreed definitions reduce mistakes before they reach decision-makers.

- Compliance made simple: Standardized processes ensure regulatory requirements are met without endless manual checks.
- Cost efficiency: Eliminating duplicated work, rework, and corrective actions saves both time and money.
- Proactive risk management: Dashboards, alerts, and monitoring make it possible to spot potential issues before they escalate.
- Better decisions: With fewer surprises and higher trust in data, strategic and operational choices are more reliable and timely.

Governance is NOT about slowing the business down. It is about **removing uncertainty**, **reducing costly mistakes**, and **making every decision count**.

Trusted data is your strongest shield.
Investing in governance today prevents risks, reduces costs, and frees your teams to focus on what drives real business value.

Looking Back From Practice

The greatest savings from governance are rarely dramatic. They are preventive.

The errors that never propagated, the decisions that never needed revisiting, the crises that never materialized.

By now, I recognize a particular kind of silence in the room during post-incident reviews. This silence follows the moment someone finally traces a costly problem back to a data decision made months earlier. The frustration in those moments is not just about the specific error. It is about how long it took to surface, and how much energy had been spent in the meantime working around a problem no one had formally owned.

What strikes me most in those reviews is rarely the size of the mistake. It is the pattern of behavior it reveals. Teams had sensed something was off. There had been quiet workarounds, information cross-checks, people recalculating numbers before important meetings "just to be sure". The signs were there. But because no one owned the problem formally, no one fixed it formally. The cost accumulated in small, invisible increments until it became undeniable.

I have also seen the reverse, and it is worth naming because it rarely gets the attention it deserves. Organizations where governance is genuinely embedded tend to have far fewer dramatic incidents. Not because they are luckier, but because issues surface earlier, when they are cheaper and easier to fix. The data steward who notices an anomaly in a weekly check, and the data owner who flags a definition conflict before it reaches a board presentation. The audit that catches a process drift before it compounds. These are not headline moments. No one writes a case study about a crisis that did not happen. But the cumulative value of those quiet non-events is real. It grows steadily over time.

The financial cost of poor data is real and measurable. But in my experience, the more significant cost is the one that never appears on a spreadsheet: the senior leader who loses confidence in the data and falls back on instinct, the initiative that stalls because no one can agree on the baseline, the decisions that are delayed for two weeks while teams reconcile numbers that should already have been aligned. These costs are diffuse, invisible, and chronic. Governance is what makes them stop accumulating.

Fewer escalations. Fewer corrections. Fewer surprises. Fewer urgent fixes. Fewer defensive behaviors. Over time, these savings grow.

Example: *An airline experienced recurring "phantom overbooking" incidents in which flights showed full in one system but had empty seats in another, resulting in denied boardings and compensation payments averaging €45,000 per month. The root cause was that four different booking systems had slightly different logic for calculating "available seats". Some counted infant lap seats, others did not; some included crew seats in the total, others did not. Each system was "correct" by its own logic, but together they created chaos. Governance did not fix the systems (that would have cost over €2M). Instead, they established a single authoritative "available seat count" rule, appointed one team to own it, and required all systems to call a central API for the calculation rather than computing it locally. Development cost: €180,000. Monthly savings from eliminated compensation: €45,000. Payback: four months. But the bigger value was invisible: customer trust* *improved, staff stress decreased, and operational teams stopped firefighting and started planning.*

Over time, teams spend less effort correcting and more effort progressing. Leaders intervene less because fewer issues reach the escalation stage. What is often overlooked is how risk reduction compounds. Each avoided failure strengthens confidence. Each clarified responsibility prevents future ambiguity.

There is something else worth saying here, and it is harder to quantify but just as real:

Governance changes the emotional texture of how organizations operate.

When people trust the data, they argue less and decide more. They spend less time in defensive mode and more time in forward-looking mode. Meetings feel different. The energy previously consumed by reconciliation is redirected toward strategy. It does not show up in a cost-benefit analysis. But anyone who has experienced both kinds of organizations, one that doubts its own numbers and one that trusts them, knows the difference immediately.

Governance pays off not through a single avoided crisis, but through many quiet non-events. That is what makes governance economically meaningful.

DAY 28

Strategic Alignments

Risk reduction protects value. Strategic alignment creates it.

Governance that is not aligned with strategy does not stay neutral. And as it drifts, it begins to generate its own gravitational pull, attracting effort, consuming capacity, and producing output that feels productive but delivers little. Standards proliferate. Metrics multiply. Forums fill calendars. Reports circulate. And somewhere in all that activity, the original question: "Whether any of this is helping the business move forward?" stops being asked.

Busy does not mean productive.

This is one of the hardest lessons in governance, and one of the most common traps. A governance team can be hardworking, committed, and genuinely disconnected from what the business actually needs, all at the same time.

This day exists to surface a hard truth: governance choices are strategic choices. What you define, measure, and protect reflects what the organization values. Governance that is not anchored to what the business is trying to achieve will drift into irrelevance. Quietly at first, then decisively.

Alignment is not about mapping governance artifacts to strategy slides. It is about ensuring that data effort supports the decisions that matter most and does not distract from them.

From the 30 Days of Data Governance Posts

Governance should not be seen as just about clean data or compliant processes. It is about **making sure data and decisions actually support your business objectives**.

Without alignment, even the best data can feel disconnected from strategy. Teams spend time analyzing, reporting, and validating data that doesn't move the needle. Strategic alignment ensures every piece of data, every process, and every insight contributes to the goals that matter most.

Here's how it shows up in practice (and back to bullet points):

- Linking data to business goals: Every dataset, dashboard, and KPI is tied to outcomes that drive value, not just numbers for numbers' sake.

- Prioritized initiatives: Governance helps focus on the areas with the highest impact, avoiding wasted effort.
- Unified understanding: Clear definitions and shared metrics ensure everyone is speaking the same language.
- Cross-functional collaboration: When business and data teams align, decisions are faster, better informed, and more confident.
- Continuous feedback: Governance frameworks provide a loop to adjust strategy as insights and circumstances evolve.

Strategic alignment transforms governance from a compliance exercise into a value driver. It is the bridge between trusted data and smart business decisions.

Governance only truly works when it is connected to what the business is trying to achieve. Alignment ensures your data investments pay off where it matters most.

Looking Back From Practice

The warning signs are recognizable once you have experienced them and know what to look for. The governance team is busy but cannot point to a decision that went better because of their work. No one really can either. The metrics are tracking well, but they never surface in leadership conversations. Standards are being maintained, but the people they are meant to help do not know they exist. Activity is present. Impact is not. This is a painful reality for many governance teams and organizations. Governance has decoupled from strategy.

Not dramatically, but through the slow accumulation of effort that points in no particular direction.

Alignment clarifies trade-offs.
And the absence of alignment quietly destroys them.

I have worked alongside governance teams that, by reasonable measure, were doing everything right. Meeting cadences were in place. Catalogs maintained. Quality dashboard green. And yet, when I sat in leadership meetings and listened to the questions being asked about customer retention, margin erosion, the market's actual profitability, and unexplained delays in deliveries, the governance work was answering none of them. The team was tracking field-level completeness scores across datasets that no one in that room had ever looked at. The gap between what governance was producing and what leadership needed had been growing quietly for many months. Nobody had noticed, because the team was visibly busy. But visible activity is not the same as useful impact.

Example: *A software company's governance team had been overwhelmed for a while. They were trying to ensure quality for 847 datasets across every department. Progress was slow, complaints were high, and leadership questioned the value. They reset by asking the executive team one question: "What are the five decisions that* *determine whether we succeed this year?" The answers were: product roadmap prioritization, sales capacity allocation, customer churn prediction, feature adoption tracking, and technical debt management. The governance team identified the 23 datasets that directly fed those five decisions and ruthlessly prioritized them. They stopped working on the other 824 datasets unless someone could demonstrate a direct link to a strategic decision. Within six months, the quality for those 23 datasets reached 95%+, strategic decisions accelerated by 40%, and executive satisfaction with data rose from 34% to 80%. They did not improve all the data; they improved the data that actually mattered.*

Alignment is not a strategy document. It is a question asked regularly and answered honestly. The question I have learned to ask governance teams early in any engagement is not "What are you working on?" but "What decisions did your work support in the last 30 days?" The answer to the first question is always long. The answer to the second is often shorter than expected and sometimes met by a pause that says more than words could. That pause is not a sign of failure. It is a sign of misalignment. And misalignment is fixable, but only once it is seen.

I have also seen the opposite, and it looks and feels entirely different. In one organization, the governance team had made a deliberate choice early on: they would only take on work that could be directly connected to a decision the business was actively trying to make. Everything else went on a waiting list. The waiting list was long. The active work was short. And the active work got done, got used, and got recognized. Governance was never questioned in that organization, not because it was invisible, but because its value was. Every initiative had a named decision behind it. Every metric had a named owner who was using it.

The contrast between those two organizations is not about capability or commitment. The teams were equally skilled, equally motivated. The difference was whether alignment had been made a deliberate practice or left to happen naturally. It does not happen naturally. It requires a recurring honest conversation between governance and leadership about what actually matters, and the discipline to stop doing things that no longer serve that purpose.

This reduces friction in day-to-day work. Teams understand why certain standards exist and others do not. Governance stops feeling arbitrary and starts feeling intentional. Over time, aligned governance reinforces strategic focus. It keeps data effort pointed in the same direction as the organization itself.

When strategy and priorities are explicit, governance becomes selective rather than exhaustive. It supports focus instead of fragmentation. Attention shifts to critical data domains, key metrics, and decision points that truly move the organization. The result is not less governance, but governance directed where it matters most.

Day 29

Building a Data-Driven Culture

Strategic alignment directs effort. Culture determines whether that effort sustains. And of the two, culture is the harder one to build because it cannot be designed into existence. It has to be earned, reinforced, and modeled repeatedly, until it becomes the way things are done rather than the way things are supposed to be done.

Before going further, it is worth being precise about **what a data-driven culture actually means**, because the phrase is used freely and defined rarely.

> *A data-driven culture is one in which data is the default input to decisions, not an optional justification for them.*

The distinction matters more than it first appears. When data is the default input, people reach for it before forming a view; they ask what the numbers show before deciding what they think. When data is the optional justification, the sequence is reversed: a position is formed first, and data is selected afterward to support it. The first creates learning; the second creates confirmation bias dressed in the language of evidence. A culture can have sophisticated dashboards, strong analytical capability, and a high data literacy, and still be operating in the second mode. The diagnostic question is not "Do we use data?" but "Do we change our minds when the data tells us to?" Organizations that can honestly answer yes to that latter question are genuinely data-driven. Most are still working towards it.

Culture is often described as a mindset, but it is revealed through behavior. It is simply how decisions are made when no one is watching.

Governance shapes those behaviors quietly: by making expectations visible, by rewarding clarity, by making good behavior easier than bad behavior, and by reinforcing what is expected, rewarded, and trusted.

The most revealing test of a data-driven culture is not what happens when data is clear and convenient. It is what happens when data is incomplete, contradictory, or tells a story nobody wants to hear. Do people surface the tension, or work around it? Do they challenge the assumptions, or protect their own version of the truth? Those moments, invisible to dashboards and governance forums, are where culture actually lives.

This day exists to connect governance to culture, not as an aspiration, but as a reinforcement mechanism, showing how the structures built over the previous 28 days of reflections quietly shape the decisions people make without thinking.

From the 30 Days of Data Governance Posts

Governance is only truly effective when it becomes part of the organizational mindset. It is not just about rules, processes, or dashboards. It is about **creating a culture where decisions are naturally guided by trusted data**.

A data-driven culture means *teams don't have to question which numbers to trust or which process to follow*. It is **embedded in daily work**, influencing decisions at every level. When everyone understands the value of accurate, reliable data, it becomes second nature to act with confidence.

Here's how it shows up in practice:

- Data in every conversation: Decisions are backed by numbers, not assumptions. Reports, dashboards, and metrics are referenced in meetings, planning sessions, and reviews.
- Shared accountability: Everyone understands their role in maintaining and using quality data. Data stewardship becomes part of the team's daily rhythm, not just a separate function.

- Open communication: Insights are discussed transparently, fostering learning, improvement, and proactive problem-solving. The connection to Day 19 is deliberate: communication is not a soft enabler of governance. It is the mechanism through which governance becomes shared rather than imposed.
- Quick adaptation: With trusted data, teams can pivot fast in response to changes, risks, or opportunities, making strategy execution more agile.
- Celebrating data wins: Recognizing examples where data-driven choices delivered real impact reinforces the culture and motivates others to follow suit.

Building a data-driven culture is a journey, not a checkbox. Governance is the **engine that powers this mindset**, ensuring data is reliable, accessible, and relevant to the decisions that matter most. Over time, it shifts behavior, builds confidence, and instills trust at every level of the organization.

Culture eats policy for breakfast.

Embedding governance into everyday behavior ensures data drives real business value.

Looking Back From Practice

Culture shifts slowly. Governance accelerates that shift by making the expectations clearer, reducing friction, and reinforcing the right choices.

But there is something governance alone cannot do. It cannot substitute for leadership that uses data visibly and genuinely. I have seen well-designed governance frameworks quietly collapse, not because of poor processes or missing roles, but because the leaders above them were not modeling the behavior they were asking others to adopt. They commissioned dashboards they never opened. They asked for data-driven decisions in town halls and then made the big calls on instinct, behind closed doors, without reference to any of it. People noticed. They always do.

When ownership is clear and consistently applied, people adapt. Issues surface earlier. Trust grows.

Example: *A professional services firm wanted to become "data-driven" but struggled with adoption. Consultants continued to rely on intuition and anecdotal client feedback rather than on analysis. The firm tried mandatory dashboard reviews and data training, but nothing stuck. We organized a strategic Decision Lab, a structured session bringing all senior leaders into the same room with one purpose: to align on what actually mattered and agree on three to five focus areas where data would make the most difference to the decisions they were already trying to make. That session did something the training had not: it made the leaders themselves choose what was worth caring about, in each other's presence. They reset by aligning incentives and recognition with those priorities. They started showcasing one "data-driven decision" at every monthly town hall, not complex analyses, but simple examples where someone used data to make a better call. A consultant shared* *that reviewing client usage patterns revealed a feature everyone thought was critical was barely used, saving six months of development time. Another showed how data on proposal win rates by industry changed their targeting strategy, increasing close rates by 19%. These were not data scientists; they were consultants who had made data part of how they worked. Within a year, "Can I show you some data on this?" became a common phrase in meetings. The shift happened not through policy, but through visible examples and social proof.*

What that firm discovered, and what holds across organizations of every kind, is that culture does not shift because a policy changes. It shifts because people see others they respect working differently. The consultants who shared their data-driven decisions at the town hall were not data champions by title. They were credible practitioners who had found that using data improved their work. That is the kind of social proof that no training program can manufacture.

I have also watched the opposite play out. In one organization I advised, the leadership team invested significantly in data literacy training across the business. Hundreds of people completed courses. Certificates were issued. A data culture program was announced with genuine fanfare. And then, six months later, I sat in an executive meeting where a major investment decision was made entirely on one person's gut feeling, while a dashboard showing directly relevant data sat open and unacknowledged on the screen behind them. Within weeks, I started hearing from people across the organization: "Why should we bother, if they don't?"

That question is the sound of a data-driven culture dying. And it dies from the top.

Governance does not create culture.
It shapes the conditions in which culture forms.

But conditions are not enough on their own. The single most powerful accelerant of a data-driven culture is leadership that walks the walk and talks the talk. Leaders who ask for data before making a decision. Who acknowledges when it changes their view. Who refer to metrics not because it is expected, but because it is how they think. When people see that behavior at the top, it becomes safe and eventually normal across the organization. Governance builds the infrastructure. Leadership makes it real.

Day 30

The Road Ahead

Most governance journeys reach an inflection point. Not a crisis; something quieter. The obvious problems are resolved. The foundation is in place. The organization has "governance."

But the path forward is less clear. Leadership attention moves to other priorities. The governance team shifts from building to sustaining, and it is not always easy to explain the value of that work to those who have forgotten what the original problem felt like.

This is where governance starts to become vulnerable. Not because it failed, but because it no longer feels urgent. The work becomes less visible. The benefits are harder to point to. What once felt essential begins to look like something that can simply keep running on its own. That is when governance begins to drift toward irrelevance.

This is the moment where many quietly lose momentum, not through failure, but by slowly letting it fade.

Day 30 exists for that moment.

Not to repeat that governance is perpetual; that has already been said often enough in this book. But to be honest about what sustainable governance actually requires: the willingness to keep asking whether what was built still fits, to adjust without abandoning, and to treat the work as something that evolves alongside the organization rather than something that was delivered to it.

Governance that stops asking those questions does not collapse. It silently becomes irrelevant. The final challenge is not whether governance was built, but whether it can keep adapting without losing its shape.

From the 30 Days of Data Governance Posts

As we wrap up this 30-day journey, let's look forward: governance is the foundation that turns data into a strategic advantage.

Good governance doesn't just protect your data or ensure compliance. It creates opportunities, drives confident decisions, and unlocks growth across the organization. When data is trusted, processes are clear, and ownership is defined, teams can innovate without fear, respond quickly to change, and focus on what matters most.

Here is how it shows up in practice:

- Continuous improvement: Governance evolves alongside the business, keeping data accurate, relevant, and actionable.
- Scalable frameworks: Policies and processes grow with the organization, enabling new initiatives without adding bottlenecks.
- Cross-team collaboration: Everyone understands their role in managing and using data, building trust and alignment.
- Informed innovation: Teams can experiment, iterate, and learn quickly because decisions are backed by reliable data.
- Long-term value: Embedding governance into everyday work transforms routine decisions into sustained business advantage.

Governance is an enabler, not a barrier. Embed it thoughtfully, and it becomes a multiplier for speed, accuracy, and growth.

Looking Back From Practice

When treated as a way of working, it becomes an advantage rather than an obligation.

If there is one thing I have changed my mind about over time, it is how much governance depends on design versus behavior. Early in my work, I believed that if the framework was clear enough with roles defined, processes mapped, and standards agreed, the organization would follow. And to some extent, it did, but not in the moments that mattered most. What I have come to see is that governance does not fail because it lacks structure. It fails where behavior is left to interpretation. The work is not only to design clarity, but to make it usable under pressure, visible in decisions, and reinforced by those people who pay attention to most. The shift from building frameworks to shaping behavior changed the way I approach governance entirely.

The organizations that benefit most from governance treat it as infrastructure. Not something that sits at the center, but something that supports everything else without drawing attention to itself. It adapts as needs change. It is maintained, not reinvented. It is questioned, but not abandoned.

What I have noticed, across organizations of very different sizes and industries, is that the ones who sustain governance past that inflection point share one habit: they never stop asking uncomfortable questions about their own framework. Not in a destabilizing way, not tearing things down for the sake of it, but with a quiet, regular honesty. Is this still working? Does this still fit? I have sat in governance reviews where the most valuable moment was not a metric going red, but a steward saying, "Actually, no one uses this process anymore," and the room having the maturity to respond with "Then let's change it" rather than "Then let's enforce it". That willingness to adjust without abandoning is what separates governance that endures from governance that eventually gets quietly bypassed.

Example: *A technology company once had excellent governance when they were 200 people. Clear roles, simple processes, trusted data. As they grew to 2,000 people across 12 countries, everything broke. They had three choices: abandon governance (too risky), freeze governance (it would stagnate), or evolve governance (hardest but necessary). They chose evolution. Every quarter, the governance council reviewed one core element: Are these roles still working? Are these definitions still clear? Do these metrics still matter? They made small adjustments continuously rather than waiting for a crisis. When they entered a new market with different privacy regulations, they adapted policies within three weeks instead of grinding to a halt. When they acquired a company, they integrated governance over six months, not six days, giving time for alignment. Five years later, at 5,000+ people, their governance was unrecognizable from day one, but it was still governance, still working, still trusted. The key was treating it as something living, not locked.*

Governance is never finished.
It matures alongside the organization.

Over time, governance becomes an advantage precisely because it no longer needs defending. People rely on it. They use it. They build from it. The destination is not implementation. It is the confidence to act.

One thing I did not include in the original series, but cannot leave out of this book, is the question now facing many organizations: how governance changes when AI enters the decision process.

Not because AI changes the principles in this book - it does not. The same questions apply. “Who is accountable for this data?” “What do these terms mean?” “Can we explain where this number comes from?” But AI changes the *stakes* of those questions in ways that are still becoming clear.

When an automated system makes decisions at speed and at scale, such as pricing, risk scoring, resource allocation, or clinical recommendations, the cost of unresolved governance does not grow linearly. It compounds. A poorly defined data element in a spreadsheet produces one wrong answer. The same poorly defined element in a model that runs ten thousand times a day produces ten thousand wrong answers, each delivered with the confidence of automation and the opacity of a system most people in the room cannot interrogate.

And when a model produces an outcome, a new governance question surfaces that frameworks rarely anticipate: “Who owns it?” Not the data, not the algorithm, but the decision that followed. Data governance does not resolve that automatically. But it is the only discipline already trained to ask.

The organizations that will navigate this well are, in my view, the ones that have already done the slower work this book describes. Not because they built an AI governance framework, but because they already know who owns their data, what their critical terms mean, and how their most important numbers are produced. That foundation does not need to be rebuilt for AI. It needs to be extended.

Governance never reaches a final state. But the groundwork laid in the previous 29 days is precisely what makes the next decade of AI-assisted decisions navigable. That is the most any governance foundation can promise, and more than most organizations currently have.

The road ahead is not shorter. But if the underlying structure is sound, it is considerably less steep because this is what governance ultimately creates: not control, but confidence in how decisions are made.

Your Turn

This final part was about making the connection between governance and the things that actually matter to leaders: speed, cost, alignment, and culture. Not as side effects of doing governance well, but the reason for doing it at all. Governance exists to serve decisions. Everything else is scaffolding. The questions below are worth returning to over time, not once, but as the organization evolves.

1. Can you name a decision that happened faster because of governance?

Not a hypothetical. A real one. If you cannot think of an example, either governance is not yet embedded in decision-making, or the connection has not been made visible. The value of governance often shows up in the meetings that did not happen, the reconciliations that were not needed, and the debates that did not start.

2. What risk has governance already prevented that leadership does not know about?

This is the quiet side of the ledger. The compliance breach that was caught early. The strategic decision made on complete rather than partial data. Governance value is often measured in non-events. Making those visible is part of the work.

3. Where is governance still experienced as overhead rather than enablement?

Honest answer only here. There is almost always somewhere. A process that creates friction without a clear benefit. A standard that no one understands the purpose of. A report that exists because it has always existed. These are worth finding and either fixing or removing. Governance that is not connected to value will eventually be worked around.

4. What does a data-driven decision look like in your organization today, and what would it look like in two years?

The gap between those two answers is essentially a governance roadmap. Not necessarily a formal one. Just an honest view of what needs to change for data to become something the organization relies on rather than debates.

Governance is not finished when you reach the end of this book. If anything, this is the point where it should start becoming clearer how organizations operate. The road ahead is not shorter, but with the right foundations, it is considerably less steep. The Conclusion offers a practical roadmap for what comes next.

Conclusion

This book opened with a question: "Can we trust our data enough to act on it?"

Thirty reflections later, the question has not gone away. It never does. What changes is the capacity to answer it, not through certainty, but through the kind of earned reliability that comes from doing the slower work: making ownership real, creating shared language, keeping quality visible, and embedding governance in how work gets done rather than layering it on top.

The organizations that get the most from governance are not the ones with the most sophisticated frameworks. They are the ones where people trust the data enough to act on it, and know who to call when they do not.

Across these thirty reflections, we have explored why that question matters, what breaks trust, and how to rebuild it systematically. Not through frameworks imposed from above, but through practices that hold in real decisions, routines, and trade-offs. It was never about perfection. It was about creating conditions where organizations can move forward with confidence: where decisions are made faster because validation is no longer needed at every step, where trust compounds rather than erodes, and where data becomes an enabler rather than a source of hesitation.

A Practical Roadmap

If you are beginning your governance journey, start with the question from Day 1: "Can we trust our data enough to act without second-guessing ourselves?" If the answer is uncertain, that hesitation is your starting point.

The six steps below are not just governance actions. They are the practical conditions that build confidence: confidence to rely on the data, confidence to make decisions without second-guessing, and confidence to move forward without unnecessary rework.

Begin with visibility, not perfection. Identify one critical decision that relies on data. Map where that data comes from, who touches it, and where trust breaks down. Do not try to fix everything - understand one thing deeply.

Establish ownership before process. Make someone accountable for that data, not in theory but in practice. Give them the mandate to resolve conflicts and the visibility to be held responsible. Ownership clarifies priorities in ways frameworks cannot.

Focus on predictability, not polish. Consistent data with known limitations is more valuable than perfect data that arrives too late. Define what "good enough" means for your context, then make that standard reliable.

Embed governance where decisions happen. Do not build governance as a separate function that reviews work after the fact.

Build it into how work gets done: into reporting, validation, hand-offs, and escalation paths.

Measure what matters, not what is easy. Track adoption, not just compliance. Measure decision speed, not just data accuracy. Monitor trust, not just technical quality. Governance succeeds when it enables action, not when it documents effort.

Iterate and adapt. Governance that worked last year may not work today. As the organization changes, revisit definitions, roles, and standards. Continuous improvement is not a phase; it is how governance stays relevant.

These six steps do not produce a finished governance program. They produce an organization that can act with confidence. One that has enough clarity to move forward, enough trust to stop second-guessing, and enough confidence to treat data as a foundation rather than a source of doubt. That is what governance is for. Not the framework. The action it makes possible.

From Governance to Confidence

Governance is not a one-off project.

Governance is not something you finish, hand over, or tick off a list. It is a way of working that evolves alongside the organization itself, shaped by the decisions, pressures, and trade-offs people face.

The true shift happens gradually. Governance moves from something people question to something they rely on. Decisions become easier because the foundations are clear. Roles are understood. Data is trusted. The organization no longer debates whether governance matters: it simply works within it.

What started as hesitation - *Can we trust our data?* - becomes confidence. Not blind faith, but earned reliability. The kind of assurance that allows organizations to move quickly because the ground beneath them is solid.

That is the real destination of this journey. Not implementation, but confidence that endures.

The goal is not to get governance right,
but to trust it enough to act.

Thank you for reading. Whether you moved through the book from beginning to end or found your way through the chapters that mattered most to you, I hope you found clarity, practical direction, and approaches that fit your context.

The work continues. But now, you have a clearer sense of where to look. And you have a map.

Governance as a Way of Working

One final reflection.

Governance never reaches a final state.

It is something organizations keep shaping through the decisions they make, the responsibilities they accept, and the way they choose to work with data.

Sustaining that takes learning, experimentation, and continuous adjustment as the organization grows and changes.

I have written this book from the perspective of someone who has spent years watching governance succeed and fail - sometimes in the same organization, sometimes in the same year. What I have come to believe is that the difference is rarely technical. It is human. Governance succeeds when people understand why it exists, feel ownership over how it works, and trust that raising issues will lead to improvement rather than punishment.

It fails when it becomes detached from people, decisions, and purpose. When it is something done to the organization instead of built with it. When the framework becomes the goal, and the goal - trusted data, confident decisions - gets lost somewhere in the documentation.

Strong governance does not eliminate complexity. It creates reliability within it. It reduces hesitation, shortens feedback loops, and replaces debate about inputs with a focus on outcomes. And it does not have to start big. In my experience, the organizations that sustain governance longest are rarely the ones that planned the most comprehensively at the start. They are the ones that started small, learned from what they built, and scaled what worked. A single-owned definition. One trusted dashboard. One team that stops arguing about numbers. That is enough to begin. The rest follows. With time, that reliability is what enables better decisions, less chaos, and more confidence across the organization.

If there is one idea to carry forward, it is this:

Governance is not about controlling data.
It is about enabling confidence.

One last thing worth noting: there is no single version of a governance team. Some organizations need a dedicated function. Others embed it across existing roles. Some start with one person and a clear mandate. What matters is not the shape; it is whether the responsibility is real, the authority is clear, and the work is connected to decisions that matter. That is how governance stops being an obligation and becomes an advantage. Where the question changes from "Can we trust the data?" to "Are we ready to act on it?"

Confidence to decide.

Confidence to act.

Confidence to grow.

Keep it simple. Keep it visible.

Keep it connected to what matters.

APPENDIX 1

The Six Parts: What Each One Builds

The book is organized into six parts, each exploring a different dimension of data governance in practice. Taken together, they show how trust is shaped, strengthened, and used in an organization.

Part 1: Why Data Governance Matters

Established the foundation. We explored why trust erodes, how poor data teaches organizations to hesitate, and why governance enters the conversation not as strategy but as a response to fatigue. The cost of bad data is not just financial; it shapes behavior, slows decisions, and creates defensive cultures.

Part 2: Building a Strong Foundation

Showed how to move from intent to structure. Roles that reflect how decisions actually get made. Standards that create consistency without chaos. Definitions that allow teams to speak the same language. Each element supports the other. None works in isolation.

Part 3: Avoiding Common Pitfalls

Surfaced the obstacles that quietly undermine governance. Silos. Manual processes that become permanent dependencies. Missing data. Conflicting sources. Inconsistent processes. These are not isolated problems; they are patterns that signal deeper misalignment.

Part 4: Embedding Governance in Daily Work

Marked the point where governance stops being extra work and starts becoming the way work gets done. Stewardship that makes responsibility real. Validation that replaces assumption with evidence. Reporting that builds confidence rather than fueling debate. Communication that creates shared understanding. Training that turns expectations into capability.

Part 5: Advanced Practices and Strategic Impact

Explored what becomes possible when the basics hold. Master data management that scales consistency. Metadata and lineage that restore transparency under scrutiny. Privacy and compliance that protect without paralyzing. Technology that amplifies maturity rather than replacing it. Continuous improvement that keeps governance relevant as the organization evolves.

Part 6: Connecting Governance to Business Value

Tied everything back to outcomes. Faster decisions because teams no longer second-guess inputs. Reduced risk because expectations are clear before they are tested. Strategic alignment because data effort supports what matters most. A data-driven culture where behavior changes not through mandate, but through consistent reinforcement of what works. The value is no longer argued for. It is visible in the outcomes.

Appendix 2

Where to Go When

This book is not a framework. It is thirty reflections from practice. Use this appendix to find a starting point, not a checklist: the right chapter is the one that speaks to the situation you are actually in.

Foundational problems - where governance usually starts

When no one agrees whose data it is → Day 2, Day 6

When two reports show different numbers → Day 8, Day 14

When data quality is inconsistent or hard to measure → Day 3, Day 10

When you suspect there are blind spots in your data → Day 13, Day 3

When data arrives late, in the wrong format, or through unclear hand-offs → Day 4, Day 12

Operational pain - governance under pressure

When people keep building workarounds → Day 11, Day 15, Day 7

When a dashboard is questioned in every meeting → Day 18, Day 8

When you cannot explain where a number came from → Day 22

When automation is being proposed → Day 12 - read this before agreeing

People and adoption - when structure exists but behavior has not changed

When stewards have been named but nothing has changed → Day 16, Day 2

When people understand the framework but do not follow it → Day 20, Day 16, Day 19

When governance adoption is low → Day 19, Day 23

Making the case - justifying and sustaining governance

When governance feels like overhead → Day 26, Day 27, Day 1

When you need to make the business case → Day 5, Day 27, Day 26

When you want to check whether governance is actually working → Day 17, Day 10

When a program has lost momentum → Day 25, Day 30

Scale and strategy - governance growing with the organization

When leadership is not engaged → Day 28, Day 10

When entering a new market or completing an acquisition → Day 25, Day 9 - read these first, Day 11

When you are about to implement MDM → Day 21, Day 9

When you are about to buy a governance tool → Day 24 - read this first

When governance is technically in place but the culture has not shifted → Day 29 - start here, Day 28, Day 20

Looking ahead

When asked how governance applies to AI → Day 22, Day 24, Day 30

APPENDIX 3

Hashtags Used in 30 Days of Data Governance

The hashtags used throughout the 30 Days of Data Governance series reflect the core themes, practices, and mindset shifts explored across the posts. They serve three purposes:

- **Orientation**: helping readers quickly understand the key domains and concepts addressed in the series.
- **Connection**: linking the content to broader professional conversations in data, information, leadership, and change.
- **Consistency**: reinforcing a shared vocabulary around modern, practical data governance.

Collected here, they provide a compact map of the governance landscape covered in the book and a reference for readers who want to explore specific topics more deeply.

Core Governance & Management

- #DataGovernance: The frameworks, roles, and practices that ensure data is managed responsibly and used effectively.
- #InformationGovernance: Governance of information across its lifecycle, including data, documents, and records.
- #InformationManagement: The practical management of information to support operations, decisions, and compliance.
- #DataManagement: The end-to-end handling of data, from creation and storage to use and retirement.
- #MasterDataManagement / #MDM / #MasterData / #MasterSource: Managing critical shared data to ensure consistency across systems.
- #InformationArchitecture / #DataArchitecture: Structuring information and data flows to support clarity and scalability.
- #DataTechnology / #GovernanceTools: Platforms and tools that support governance, quality, and oversight.

Data Quality, Trust & Transparency

- #DataQuality: Ensuring data is fit for purpose and supports reliable outcomes.
- #TrustedData / #TrustInData / #DataTrust: Confidence that data can be relied upon for decisions.
- #Accuracy: Data correctly reflects reality.
- #Completeness: Required data is present and not missing.
- #Consistency: Data aligns across systems and contexts.
- #Timeliness: Data is available when needed.

- #MissingData: Gaps in data that impact quality and decisions.
- #CostOfBadData: The financial and operational impact of poor data quality.
- #DataTransparency: Visibility into where data comes from and how it is used.
- #DataLineage: Tracing data from source to consumption.
- #Metadata: Contextual information that explains data meaning and usage.

Ownership, Roles & Accountability

- #DataOwnership / #DataOwner: Clear accountability for data assets.
- #DataStewardship / #DataSteward: Operational responsibility for maintaining data quality and standards.
- #Accountability: Ownership of decisions, data outcomes, and governance practices.
- #DataAudit: Reviewing data controls and usage.
- #DataValidation: Ensuring data meets defined rules and expectations.

Strategy, Leadership & Business Value

- #DataStrategy: Aligning data initiatives with business objectives.
- #DataLeadership / #DataLeader: Leading data as a strategic organizational capability.
- #Leadership: Guiding people and organizations through governance and change.

- #BusinessValue: Tangible benefits created through effective data practices.
- #BusinessGrowth: Using data to enable scale and informed growth.
- #Innovation: Enabling new ideas and capabilities through trusted data.
- #RiskManagement: Reducing operational, regulatory, and strategic risk.
- #CostEfficiency: Lowering costs through better data practices.

Decision-Making & Alignment

- #DataDriven / #DataDrivenDecisions: Using data as a foundation for decisions.
- #BusinessDecisions: Decisions supported by reliable information.
- #BusinessAlignment: Ensuring data efforts support business priorities.
- #SingleSourceOfTruth: A trusted, shared reference for critical data.
- #ConflictingSources: Multiple data versions creating confusion.
- #DataAlignment: Harmonizing data across teams and systems.
- #DataKPIs / #DataMetrics: Measuring governance, quality, and impact.
- #FollowSmartMetrics: Using meaningful, actionable measurements.

Processes, Ways of Working & Improvement

- #DataProcesses / #ProcessManagement: Embedding governance into daily workflows.
- #ProcessOptimization: Improving efficiency and clarity in data-related processes.
- #DataFlows: How data moves across systems and organizations.
- #ContinuousImprovement: Iteratively strengthening governance maturity.
- #GovernanceMaturity: The evolution of governance capability over time.
- #Framework: Structured approaches to governance and quality.
- #ConsistencyWithoutChaos: Standardization that supports, not blocks, the business.

People, Culture & Change

- #DataCulture: Shared values and behaviors around data.
- #ChangeManagement: Supporting people through governance and data change.
- #Collaboration: Cross-functional cooperation around data.
- #Communication: Making governance clear, relevant, and accessible.
- #Training: Building skills and understanding.
- #Awareness: Creating shared understanding of data responsibilities.
- #SystematicLearning: Continuous learning embedded into governance practices.

Standards, Definitions & Language

- #DataDefinitions: Clear, shared meanings of key data elements.
- #DataGlossary: A common vocabulary for data across the organization.
- #SpeakingTheSameLanguageAcrossTeams: Reducing friction through shared understanding.
- #DataStandard / #DataPolicy: Agreed rules guiding how data is managed.

Compliance, Privacy & Ethics

- #DataPrivacy: Protecting personal and sensitive data.
- #Compliance: Meeting legal, regulatory, and internal requirements.

Community, Identity & Series-Specific

- #30DaysOfDataGovernance: The core series and learning journey this book is based on.
- #AKLYON: My consulting practice, behind the perspectives and experience shared.
- #AskMeAboutDataGovernance: Invitation to dialogue and shared learning.
- #AskMeAboutRunning: A personal nod to endurance, discipline, and long-term thinking.

About the Author

Karima Makrof has spent over two decades in the rooms where data governance either quietly works or quietly breaks down.

Across financial services, logistics, retail, manufacturing, and technology, she has worked alongside leadership teams, data offices, architects, and operational staff - as advisor, leader, and embedded practitioner. The pattern she kept seeing was rarely about missing frameworks or absent ambition. It was about blurred ownership, uneven trust in the numbers, and governance that lived in documents rather than decisions.

She later founded her own advisory company, and continues that work with leaders and teams navigating a wide range of governance challenges: from establishing accountability structures that actually hold to rebuilding confidence in data that has quietly lost it.

Her approach is practical and clear-eyed, grounded in the reality of how organizations function under pressure, not how governance manuals say they should. She has learned to distrust complexity that exists to signal effort rather than create clarity.

She is also an endurance athlete, which may explain the instinct for discipline, the long view, and the refusal to look for shortcuts where there are none.

The Confidence to Act grew out of her "30 Days of Data Governance" LinkedIn series and reflects everything that practice taught her about what breaks and what holds.

Index

accountability, 22, 43, 103, 157, 207
adaptability, 176, 179, 180, 208
adoption, 52, 63, 107, 133, 169, 175, 176, 205, 223
AI, 161, 162, 174, 218, 219, 236
analysis, 34, 105, 198, 209
analyst, 24, 33, 35, 55, 78, 173, 190
analytics, 24, 71, 153, 171
audit, 123–125, 145
automation, 91–94, 169
bureaucracy, 57, 81, 109, 188
business value, 11, 185, 187, 193, 205, 231
change management, 19, 107, 169, 205
Chief Data Officer (CDO), 88, 137
Chief Financial Officer (CFO), 105, 155, 160
collaboration, 57, 85, 133, 134–135, 157, 201, 213
communication, 63, 115, 133–137, 145, 205, 231
compliance, 163–166, 195
confidence, 11, 21, 31, 47, 99, 151, 157, 187, 223, 228
conflicting sources, 103–105, 107, 113
cost, 43–45, 193–196
culture, 120, 185, 205–207
dashboards, 129–131, 206
data asset, 171, 172, 174, 239
data catalog, 169, 172, 174
data champion, 51, 205
data ecosystem, 157
data element, 108, 218, 242
data flow, 37–38, 43, 57, 69, 85, 107
Data Governance (DG), 11, 19, 21, 49, 83, 103, 115, 129, 133, 139, 169, 187
data literacy, 206, 210
data management, 140, 171
data owner, 27–29, 52, 177
data quality, 31–32, 76, 129, 176, 191
data silos, 85–87, 104
data standard, 60
data steward, 117–120, 207
data-driven, 103, 185, 205–207, 221, 231
data-driven culture, 205, 211, 233
decision-making, 31, 65, 187, 221
definitions, 64–66, 151, 169
encryption, 166
ethics, 242

framework, 11, 117, 133, 223
General Data Protection Regulation (GDPR), 166
glossary, 64, 65, 66, 67, 71, 76, 77
information architecture, 38, 59, 70, 71, 76
Key Performance Indicator (KPI), 76, 77, 82, 86, 130, 189, 200
leadership, 76, 123, 202, 209
lineage, 155–158
Machine Learning (ML), 162, 174
Master Data Management (MDM), 151, 152, 153, 154, 155, 181, 236, 238
maturity, 75, 91, 151, 152, 169, 170, 175, 181, 231
metadata, 155–158
metrics, 73–77, 201
ownership, 22, 31, 43, 103, 151, 193, 223
policies, 57–58, 118, 177
privacy, 163–165, 169
reliability, 25, 109, 223
reporting, 75, 103, 129–130, 145, 157, 187, 199, 200, 223
risk, 85, 163, 193–195, 199
roadmap, 203, 224
roles and responsibilities, 51–53, 177
stewardship, 115–118, 207
strategy, 119, 185, 202, 208
training and awareness, 27, 51, 139–141
transparency, 124, 130, 157, 161, 163, 232
trust, 11, 31, 51, 103, 129, 157, 193, 223
trustworthy, 22, 76, 163
validation, 123–125, 145, 187

www.ingramcontent.com/pod-product-compliance
Lightning Source LLC
LaVergne TN
LVHW022202200926
848481LV00006B/1813